JOHN
GIELGUD

JOHN GIELGUD

AN ACTOR'S LIFE

GYLES BRANDRETH

SUTTON PUBLISHING

First published in 2000 by
Sutton Publishing Limited · Phoenix Mill
Thrupp · Stroud · Gloucestershire · GL5 2BU
Revised and expanded from *John Gielgud: A Celebration*, 1984

Reprinted in 2000

British Library Cataloguing in Publication Data
A catalogue record for this book is available from the British
Library

ISBN 0 7509 2690 2

Typeset in 11/16 pt Photina.
Typesetting and origination by
Sutton Publishing Limited.
Printed and bound in England by
J.H. Haynes & Co. Ltd, Sparkford.

CONTENTS

PREFACE

This book offers a brief account of one of the most extraordinary careers in the history of entertainment. John Gielgud made his first appearance at the Old Vic Theatre in London in 1921, his first radio broadcast in 1923, his first film in 1924. By 1926 he was starring in the West End. In 1928 he made his debut on Broadway. Through eight decades his was a household name. Harcourt Williams produced Gielgud's first King Lear in 1931. Kenneth Branagh produced his last, a special radio production marking Sir John's ninetieth birthday on 14 April 1994.

In the 1920s John Gielgud was making silent pictures. Half a century later he emerged as one of the world's most sought-after movie actors. After winning his first Oscar for *Arthur* at the age of seventy-eight, he appeared in dozens of films and television series. He was working until only a few months before his death, aged ninety-six, on 21 May 2000. Inevitably, there are millions who have only ever seen him on screen, but it is as stage actor that he would want to be remembered, above all, as an interpreter of Shakespeare. 'Never has English sounded more beautiful from the human mouth', was the verdict on his Hamlet at Elsinore in 1939.

John Gielgud was the giant of twentieth-century theatre, but also one of the most generous and amusing of men. I wouldn't presume to say I was a friend: simply one of his biographers, a grateful audience and occasional prompt – not that Sir John needed much prompting. He loved to talk, he loved to gossip. Despite the perfect posture and aristocratic demeanour that made him seem so self-assured, and somewhat grand and forbidding, he was a shy, sensitive man, keenly aware of, and inclined to exaggerate, his own shortcomings. When I first worked with him, in the early 1970s, he came to record the narration for a *son et lumière* I was directing. His reading was impeccable, his instinctive phrasing flawless, the shading exactly what was required, but he wasn't happy. 'I'm afraid I'm letting you down badly,' he kept saying. 'We'd better start all over again.'

However self-deprecating he may have been at times, and whatever the public and critical reaction to his performances, Gielgud's overall attitude to his work was, from start to finish, one of total dedication. His commitment to his craft was all-absorbing and absolute. Peter Brook described Gielgud's mind as 'unique and endlessly inventive . . . he had only one reference: an intuitive sense of quality.' Unlike some other fine players in the older actor-manager tradition (and unlike his near-contemporary, Donald Wolfit), Gielgud always sought to surround himself with the best. From the early 1930s to the mid-1970s he worked almost as much as a director as an actor. Some said that all too often, when directing a play in which he was also appearing, his concern for the production overall was at the expense of his own performance. In a business not noted for those qualities, Gielgud was neither a selfish actor nor a jealous one.

I am happy to say Sir John approved of the books I published about him. He did not like all the pictures I selected. He was particularly unhappy with a drawing of him at seventy by David Hockney ('If I really thought I looked like that I'd kill myself tomorrow'), which is why it does not feature among the illustrations here. Sir John approved of my text, and corrected some of the detail. I think he particularly liked the way I tried to tell the story of his working life through the words and recollections of people who saw him in performance – friends, colleagues, even critics. Generously, he claimed to be content with the words of his that I had chosen to use ('Gyles – You are quoting a few of the only fairly intelligent things I have ever said about the theatre – thank you!'), and I know he liked the way – while, of course, covering his career as a film and television actor and, inevitably, touching on his private life – I tried to concentrate on Gielgud as a man of the theatre. 'The theatre has been my universe,' he said to me. 'I am useless at almost everything except where the theatre is concerned. I have no family. I don't have the urge to take holidays in the way other people do. I read, I walk, I watch TV, but I don't like to be idle. I have had my fill of parties and great social gatherings. I no longer crave for success and acclaim as once I did. I feel useless unless I have a job, but when I am working I am at ease with myself. To work in the theatre is all I have ever wanted to do. Acting has rid me of my frustrations and satisfied me of many of my ambitions. It is more than an occupation or a profession; for me it has been a life.'

ACKNOWLEDGEMENTS

In telling the story of John Gielgud's career, wherever possible I have used the words of eyewitnesses. I have quoted most of the leading critics of the day and many of Sir John's colleagues and friends, and, where appropriate, I am grateful to the authors and publishers of the books listed in the bibliography for permission to reproduce extracts from them. I am grateful too for the contributions garnered in conversation with Eileen Atkins, Kenneth Branagh, Richard Briers, Constance Cummings, Noel Davis, Edward Fox, Clive Francis, Dulcie Gray, the late Sir Alec Guinness, Sir Peter Hall, David Hemmings, Sheridan Morley, James Roose-Evans, John Schlesinger, Paul Scofield and Sir Donald Sinden. The early part of the chronology of Sir John's stage appearances is based on the one in *These Our Actors* by Richard Findlater (1983) and the chronology of his film and television appearances was compiled with the help of the British Film Institute and Sir John's agents at the time of his death, International Creative Management. My quotations from Sir John are taken from my conversations with him, his own published reminiscences and from a wide variety of interviews given by him since 1932, especially those given by him to John Boothe and Lewis Funke, Cyril Butcher, Gerald Clarke, John Cornwell, Derek Hart, Harold Hobson, Julie Kavanagh, Peter Roberts, George Rylands. Above all, of course, I am grateful to Sir John himself for the permission generously given to me to reproduce copyright material and personal photographs.

one

'WONDERFUL ACTOR, WONDERFUL FRIEND'
1904–2000

The first time I saw John Gielgud on stage, the audience booed. It was 1963, the opening night of Thornton Wilder's *The Ides of March* at the Theatre Royal, Haymarket, with Sir John as a modern-dress Julius Caesar. It was not a success. When I first met the great actor not long afterwards (I was twenty, a star-struck Oxford undergraduate; he was sixty-five, the acclaimed leader of his profession), he asked me what I had seen him in. I told him. 'Oh dear,' he sighed, 'Were you really there? I am so sorry. It was terrible, truly terrible. I went through a bad patch, you know. I've had one or two.' Not many.

I am fairly familiar with the highs and lows of his extraordinary career. With his blessing, I published two accounts of it during his lifetime and, over thirty years, I was privileged to spend many memorable hours sitting, notebook in hand, gazing at that noble countenance, listening to the Gielgud voice – 'all cello and woodwind', in Kenneth Tynan's phrase – as, effortlessly, and at an alarming pace, Sir John rattled off anecdote after anecdote. He could talk for an hour without pause. As I scribbled I looked up at him, but he rarely looked at me. As a story reached its pay-off – every tale appeared beautifully crafted – his eyes would slide to one side and he'd glance my way to see that I was suitably amused – or moved. (Alongside a waspish sense of humour, he had a profoundly sentimental streak. Famously, he could cry at will. 'It's rather a cheap effect. I know I shouldn't do it. If the actor cries, the audience doesn't.'†) Always immaculately turned out, with ramrod back and Turkish cigarette permanently in hand, he was an odd mix of Edwardian dandy and Roman emperor, gossip and grandee. He performed his stories not to me, I felt, but to an invisible audience in the middle distance.

To get on with Sir John, to understand him at all, you had to share his love of the theatre. It was his life. In 1983, the year before Gielgud's eightieth birthday, the playwright Ronald Harwood went to see Sir Ralph Richardson, then eighty-one, in the hope of coaxing from him some reminiscences of his old friend and colleague. Richardson liked to smoke a pipe and showed Harwood a beautiful silver tobacco jar he had been given. 'Johnny gave me that,' he said. 'He's given me so many things. Gave us some glorious silver for our silver wedding, so that whenever we dine – there's Johnny. He's everywhere in this

---

† That isn't always true. The actress Joyce Grenfell recalled going to the Theatre Royal, Haymarket, to see Gielgud's programme of Shakespearean readings, *The Ages of Man*: 'The beauty of his voice moves me so terribly that I was looking through tears. So was he. I never saw a man cry so much. A lounge suit isn't right for Lear. Better when I closed my eyes. Not that any of that matters. He is a giant, and he does make me see the horses "printing their proud hoofs i' the receiving earth".'

house. I think of him often. Wonderful actor. Wonderful friend. Never known a man so keen on the theatre. Extraordinary. I've had lunch with Johnny and the moment I mention something that isn't to do with the theatre, he goes blank. Gets that bored look . . . so I've taken to saying things on purpose just to get the reaction. The other day I told him Concorde flies faster than sound. On cue, the bored look. Wonderful fellow.'

Gielgud was a voracious reader of newspapers and magazines – 'And potboilers: I read the most dreadful rubbish' – but professed no interest in world affairs or domestic politics. Not long before his death he confessed to me, 'I have lost all interest in the London mayoral race now that Glenda [Jackson] is out of the running. She was a wonderful Cleopatra, you know. She'd have been a splendid Lady Mayoress.'

Whatever the subject under discussion, he always came back to the theatre. Ronald Harwood tells a story of Gielgud and another actor playing in the same film, sitting on the set in their canvas chairs, waiting to be called for their next shot. Sir John was reading; the other actor, wrestling with *The Times* crossword, leant over to Gielgud and asked, 'Sorry, but is there a character in Shakespeare called the Earl of Westmoreland?' 'Yes,' murmured Sir John, without looking up, 'in *Henry IV Part Two.*' Then, to break the bad news, he looked up, 'But it's a very poor part.'

Doing the crossword in *The Times* was the nearest Sir John ever got to regular exercise. 'I loathe sport,' he told me gleefully, 'detest it. I do no exercise, I never have. You know, Olivier used to work so hard to prepare himself for his roles. I was rather jealous of the trouble he used to take. When he did his famous Othello, he went into training for months on end, lifting weights, going for long runs, swimming up and down his pool for hours at a stretch. He succeeded in altering his whole physique, the way he walked, the range of his voice. Quite extraordinary. My Othello was not a success and his was. Is there a lesson there? Very possibly,' he said, his eyes twinkling, 'but the truth is I'm very lazy, I've never bothered with that kind of thing. No exercise, and I don't diet. I eat what I like, and I enjoy wine. I enjoy smoking too. I always have. I smoke furiously, at least a packet a day. Smoking, I suppose, is one of my principal pleasures.'

All I ever heard Gielgud talk about with any enthusiasm was the world of entertainment. 'You must understand that cast adrift in the ordinary world I am a timid, shy, cowardly man, but once I go into the theatre I have great authority and I get great respect and love from all the people working in it . . . It is where I belong.' I asked him if there had ever been a prospect of him doing something else: 'No. My parents hoped I might become an architect, but I was besotted with the theatre as far back as I can remember. As you know, as a boy, I took lessons from Lady Benson. She said I walked "like a cat with rickets", but I persisted. I went to RADA.† There really wasn't anything else I wanted to do. Or could.'

As with the other 'greats' of his vintage – Donald Wolfit (1902–68), Ralph Richardson (1902–83), Laurence Olivier (1907–89), Peggy Ashcroft (1907–91), Michael Redgrave (1908–85) – it was to the formidable Lilian Baylis (1874–1937), manager of Sadler's Wells and the Old Vic, that he owed the break that established him as a classical actor of

---

† The Royal Academy of Dramatic Art, founded in 1904, the year of Gielgud's birth, by the actor-manager Sir Herbert Beerbohm Tree (1853–1917).

the first rank. 'She could be rather fierce, you know. She was terribly devout. And utterly determined. I must say she kept us on our toes.'

At the Old Vic, in a period of just twenty months between 1929 and 1931, Gielgud's roles included Romeo, Richard II, Oberon, Mark Antony, Orlando, Macbeth, Hotspur, Prospero, Antony, Malvolio, Benedick, King Lear, and the first of his celebrated Hamlets. 'I was very young. I simply threw myself at the part like a man learning to swim and I found the text would hold me up if I sought the truth in it.'

When I last saw Sir John I asked him to name a favourite performance. He simply shook his head and closed his eyes. I know he had a particular place in his heart for Gordon Daviot's *Richard of Bordeaux*, 1933 ('My first "smash hit". There were queues around the block. Quite wonderful.') and for the successes he enjoyed on stage in the 1970s with Sir Ralph Richardson ('Dear Ralph. Dear, dear Ralph.') Outside Shakespeare, he had a special fondness for John Worthing in *The Importance of Being Earnest* and Sir Joseph Surface in *The School for Scandal*. Laurence Olivier called it 'the best light comic performance I've ever seen, or ever shall.'

Sir John said (in a way Olivier might not have done): 'I am lacking in ambition for power, large sums of money or a passionate desire to convince other people that they are wrong or I am right, but I have a violent and sincere wish to be a good craftsman and to understand what I try to do in the theatre, so as to be able to convince the people I work with.' Rightly, the obituaries published after his death on 21 May 2000 celebrated Gielgud as the great interpreter of Shakespeare, but to people of my generation, born after the Second World War, it is in modern work that he will best be remembered.

Aged ninety-five, in 1999, his last professional engagement was to be in a piece by Samuel Beckett. Aged fifty-four, in 1958, he was asked to play in the British premiere of Beckett's *Endgame*. He told me he turned the offer down because he hated the play, 'really hated it': he yearned to be in something 'modern', he wanted to be 'in vogue', but 'Beckett back then simply wasn't for me. Most of it I couldn't understand and what I did comprehend I didn't like.'

The sense of being out of touch ('I was old hat for quite a while, you know'), unable to relate to the writers of his time, lasted for several unnerving years from the mid-1950s, really, until 1968, when, aged sixty-four, he accepted the part of the Headmaster in Alan Bennett's play-cum-revue *Forty Years On*. 'It was hardly avant-garde, it was a nostalgic pastiche', but it was the vehicle that brought him back into the vanguard. It led him to the then home of 'new writing', the Royal Court Theatre in London's Sloane Square, and to playing with Ralph Richardson in David Storey's *Home* (directed by Lindsay Anderson) and, later, Harold Pinter's *No Man's Land* (directed by Peter Hall) – for many the definitive modern Gielgud performances.

In 1984, when I published my first account of Sir John's career, Lindsay Anderson wrote to me, questioning my chronic enthusiasm for *No Man's Land* (I saw the production three times): 'You won't be surprised to hear that I disagree when you say that John and Ralph's collaboration in *No Man's Land* had "a magical dimension that their earlier stage encounters had lacked". "An obtrusive virtuosity" *I'd* have said . . . But then I've never been able to understand the enthusiasm aroused by pretentious but essentially hollow pieces like *No Man's Land* and I can think of several others.

Really, you know, I think the turning point in John's career in the sixties was his appearance in *The Charge of the Light Brigade*. It made him feel for the first time that he could act successfully on film – and he got on so well with Tony Richardson that he lost his fear and suspicion of the Sloane Square "avant-garde".'

The affection between Gielgud and Tony Richardson, who directed *The Charge of the Light Brigade* (and who, at the Royal Court, had directed the original productions of John Osborne's *Look Back in Anger* and *The Entertainer*), was mutual. John Gielgud, said Tony Richardson, 'is quite simply the nicest, most human actor I've ever worked with, and, together with Jack Nicholson, the most intelligent. John adores the theatre, theatre gossip, actors, actresses – he is steeped in them – but he equally adores books, poetry, music, films, travel. What he likes delights him, and he can delight you with his delight. And what he loathes he can amuse you with. He is a constant responder, a constant enjoyer. That is what has kept him so perpetually young, and perhaps is why he has outlasted so many of his great contemporaries who have fallen by the wayside.'

On Gielgud's eightieth birthday, I organised a party in his honour at the Old Vic. I persuaded the actor Christopher Reeve to bring on the birthday cake. 'Oh,' cooed Sir John, 'Superman. Thank you, Gyles. You really have thought of *everything*.' I got the impression that Sir John was quite comfortable with his own homosexuality. His manner, the stories he told, the way in which he told them, the company he kept – all suggested (at least from the late 1960s when I knew him) that he accepted his sexuality without either anxiety or remorse, and expected that others would know of it and accept it too. It was not something he discussed. As a rule, people of his generation did not. He was brought up (in Kenneth Williams' memorable phrase) 'long before the-love-that-dare-not-speak-its-name started shouting the odds from the rooftops'. He guarded his privacy. He stopped allowing journalists to come to his home ('Invasion of one's private life really is rather trying, don't you agree?'), but not because he was unduly secretive or because he was hypocritical. He believed in discretion (and good manners) and felt that if the public knew too much about 'you as a person' it could get in the way of their 'appreciation of your work'.

Sir John told me, without much conviction, that there had once been the possibility of his marrying Lillian Gish, the American silent film star and actress who played Ophelia to his Hamlet on Broadway in 1936. She was beautiful, they enjoyed each other's company, but she was eleven years his senior and, frankly, I do not believe Gielgud was ever the marrying kind. Sir Harold Hobson, drama critic of the *Sunday Times* from 1947 to 1976 and 'a good friend' of Gielgud's since the 1920s, marked the great actor's eightieth birthday with a bizarre essay regretting the fact that Gielgud had never married:[†] 'Marriage steadies a man. Gielgud's career has certainly been erratic; it could well have done with that bit of steadying and of common sense which a wife may bring. It has reached some tremendous heights

---

† It appeared in *The Ages of Gielgud*, edited by Ronald Harwood, in 1984. Lindsay Anderson wrote to me: 'How foolish of Harwood to have included that insane piece by Harold Hobson: but then I don't imagine that either he or Hobson have much sense of humour, or grace.' Hobson I hardly knew; Harwood is funny and delightful.

more than once, and also fallen to some sickening depths. A touch of regularity would have saved a lot of unhappiness.'

Gielgud met the first serious love of his life in 1926 when he was appearing in *The Constant Nymph* at the New Theatre (now the Albery) in St Martin's Lane. John Perry was a young actor, 'not very good, I am afraid' (according to Sir John). 'He was Irish, from a well-to-do family, very handsome and charming. Very witty too. He loved gambling and the pleasures of the turf.' Perry (known as John P) and Gielgud (John G) lived together until Perry met and fell for the true love of his life, the celebrated producer, managing director of H.M. Tennent, and doyen of the West End from the 1930s to the 1960s, Hugh 'Binkie' Beaumont. Gielgud had a number of other relationships and liaisons, none of which he advertised, not only because of his natural discretion, but also because, for two-thirds of his long life, male homosexual acts were a criminal offence.

John Gielgud was born in 1904, only nine years after the imprisonment of Oscar Wilde and sixty-three years before the decriminalisation of 'homosexual acts between consenting adults in private'. In 1953, shortly after receiving his knighthood in the Coronation Honours List, he was humiliated publicly when he was arrested and fined £10 for 'persistently importuning male persons for an immoral purpose'. He feared the incident and the scandal that followed (complete with outraged editorials in the *Sunday Express* and elsewhere) might end his career. It didn't, but it shocked many of his admirers (and some of his colleagues), created difficulty the following year when he hoped to appear in the United States, and caused him to be blackballed as a potential member of the Garrick Club – despite being proposed by Laurence Olivier and Alec Guinness. In time, all was forgotten and forgiven: Sir John joined the Garrick in 1970; he became a Companion of Honour in 1977 and was appointed to the Order of Merit in 1996.

For the last forty years of his life, Gielgud shared his home with one man, Martin Hensler, 'a master gardener', twenty years his junior, Hungarian by birth. From the end of the war until the mid-1970s, Gielgud lived at 16 Cowley Street, a small, elegant, terraced house in Westminster. In 1973, encouraged by Hensler, he bought South Pavilion at Wotton Underwood, near Aylesbury, in Buckinghamshire, a seventeenth-century pavilion, with glorious gardens and 'wonderful capabilities'. Hensler masterminded the restoration and redecoration of the house and the recreation of the classical garden, turning the whole into what Alec Guinness called 'John and Martin's stately pleasure dome'. At Sir John's eightieth birthday lunch, he said to me, 'I wish I had settled down and moved to the country years ago. I am not sure that living in Cowley Street was a good idea, too many temptations. You know when Oscar Wilde was cross-examined about that part of town – it was quite notorious in his day – he said, "I don't know about it being a disreputable neighbourhood. I do know it is near the Houses of Parliament."'†

---

† Sir John had a fund of Wilde stories, but he was frustrated that Lord Alfred Douglas, whom he had met but not taken to, had nothing very memorable to tell him about Wilde. 'He was somewhat bitter and unpleasant, very full of himself. He would boast about his friendship with Wilde, but when I asked him about the original production of *The Importance of Being Earnest* he could tell me nothing about it. He did not seem to recollect it at all.'

In April 1994, when I was a member of parliament, I invited Sir John to join me and my wife and the actress-turned-MP Glenda Jackson for lunch at the House of Commons to celebrate his ninetieth birthday. He arrived in Central Lobby at one, on the dot, twinkling and cherubic, amazingly upright and steady.

'It's a great honour that you should join us, Sir John,' I said.

'Oh, I'm delighted to have been asked,' he murmured. 'You see, all my real friends are dead.' (He had a legendary capacity for the accidental insult. You will find examples peppered through the pages that follow. I have kept my favourites for the final chapter.)

That day – actually, every day, certainly every time I ever met him – the stories just poured out of him. He had known everybody. He had seen them all, from Sarah Bernhardt to Ralph Fiennes. (While the best of his stories came from the past, he took pride in being fully up to speed on the latest plays, films, performances.) We talked about his times in New York. 'Marlene [Dietrich] invited me to hear her new record. We gathered round the gramophone, and when we were settled the record was put on. It was simply an audience applauding her! We sat through the entire first side and then we listened to the other side: more of the same!'

He talked about his famous production of *The Importance of Being Earnest*. 'When we went to America, Margaret [Rutherford] moved up to play Lady Bracknell instead of Edith [Evans].'

'Why didn't Dame Edith play the part in New York?'

'She was introduced to a blind devotee of the theatre who heard her speak and said to her, "You are much too beautiful to play Lady Bracknell", and that was that. Edith was very much concerned about her beauty, you know. Margaret agreed to move up from Miss Prism to play Lady Bracknell on condition she could model her performance entirely on Edith's. It was typically modest of her.' (Pause. Sip of wine. Twinkle.) 'Of course, Margaret's Lady Bracknell was very much the Lady Mayoress to Edith's Queen Mary.'

That prompted Queen Mary stories. 'Queen Mary herself enjoyed the theatre. King George enjoyed his playgoing at the back of the box, chatting about racing with Sir Edward Elgar. They went to a matinee of *Hamlet* at the Haymarket and the Queen enquired at what time the performance was due to end. "You see, the King always has to have his tea punctually, and he is so anxious not to miss the girl with straws in her hair."'

Sir John's favourite Queen Mary story started with King George out walking in the garden of Buckingham Palace and asking why his customary equerry was not in attendance. He was told the man was unwell. 'What's wrong with him?' asked the King. 'Oh, the universal complaint, sir,' was the guarded reply. Next day Queen Mary remarked to someone, 'I hear His Majesty's equerry is ill. What's the matter with him?' 'A bad attack of haemorrhoids, I'm afraid, ma'am.' 'Oh,' said the Queen, 'why did the King tell me it was the clap?'

Sir John loved a wicked story. He had a wicked sense of humour. The actor David Hemmings appeared with him in *The Charge of The Light Brigade* in the 1960s: 'Sir John was so charming and so funny. There was a wholly inaccurate rumour that the film's director, Tony Richardson, was having an affair with our leading lady, Jill Bennett. We were on location, filming in the Anatolian plane. Jill was in her tent while the rest of us, Sir John included, were standing around the coffee urns waiting for the next set-up. Tied up near the tent was a Russian dancing bear that somehow managed to free itself and, before any of us could do anything about it, went lumbering towards Jill's tent and got tangled up in the guy ropes. Poor Jill came rushing out of the tent, pursued by this enormous bear. Sir John looked up and cried, "Oh, Mr Richardson, how could you! And in your motoring-coat too!"'

At the ninetieth birthday lunch Sir John's conversational cast list included Orson Welles, Micheal MacLiammoir (was it MacLiammoir or Welles who kept a flashlight up his sleeve so he could illuminate his face on the darkened stage? I can't remember), Kenneth Branagh ('so clever and so delightful'), Peter Brook ('so very clever – but oh dear . . .'), Donald Wolfit ('He hated me, *hated* me. The feeling was entirely mutual').

He was extraordinary – and he was ninety. I said to him, 'After lunch, would you like to come to Prime Minister's Questions?'

He grinned. 'I've been before. As I recall, last time Mr Bonar Law was answering the questions.'

'Do come again. I know the Prime Minister [John Major] is hoping to pay a small tribute to you.'

'Oh, no, no,' he looked quite alarmed. 'I think I might find that a little embarrassing. I'll just slip away quietly, if you don't mind. I don't want any fuss. I think a clean exit is so important, don't you?' As we were walking back across Central Lobby, he paused and smiled and fluted gently, 'This has been great fun. Thank you. I have had a very lucky life.'

I rather think we were the lucky ones.

two

ARTHUR JOHN GIELGUD
1904–1929

John Gielgud was born in Kensington, London, on 14 April 1904. His father, Frank Gielgud, was a successful stock-broker, very much the comfortable Edwardian, despite the fact that he was of Lithuanian descent and only a second generation Londoner. Frank's father was born in England, and worked at the War Office and as a foreign correspondent, but his grandparents were Polish. One of Frank's grandmothers was an acclaimed Polish actress called Aniela Aszpergerowa. One of his grandfathers was a Polish cavalry officer called John Gielgud and it was this John Gielgud who left Poland for England in the 1830s.

Our John Gielgud's first name was actually Arthur. He was named after his maternal grandfather, Arthur Lewis, but the Arthur was soon dropped in favour of his second name and he was known as John, or Jack, to his family from an early age. His mother, Kate, belonged to one of the most distinguished of all theatrical clans: the Terrys. Her immediate family included at least twenty individuals closely concerned with the theatre, of whom the best known were probably her mother, Kate Terry, her uncle, Fred Terry, her aunt, Ellen Terry, and her cousins Gordon Craig and Phyllis Neilson-Terry.

Young John was delighted with his celebrated relations: 'I was enormously englamoured by my family, particularly the ones who were still acting when I was a boy. My parents didn't encourage this very much, although they were naturally very proud of it too. My mother was the theatrical one because she was a Terry; but my father, who was partly Polish, had a curious, practical, middle-class English realism, mixed with a certain romantic panache.' John was the third of Kate and Frank Gielgud's four children, all of whom were 'tremendously theatrically minded'. They spent hours dressing up and playing acting games, and their toy theatre – with a most ambitious and imaginative repertoire of home-made plays glorying in such titles as *Plots in the Harem, Lady Fawcett's Ruby* and *Kill That Spy* – absorbed and entertained them for much of their childhood.

John's formal education began when he followed his older brothers Lewis and Val to Hillside, a prep school in Godalming, Surrey, where his academic career was not especially distinguished but where he was able to make his dramatic debut before a real audience. His first public performance was in the role of the Mock Turtle in a school production of *Alice in Wonderland*. 'I sang "Soup of the Evening" with increasing volume and shrillness in each verse.' Having given the Hillside boys, parents and teachers his Mock Turtle, he followed it up with his Humpty Dumpty, his Shylock and his Mark Antony. In April 1999, at the time of Sir John's ninety-fifth birthday, I received a letter from one of his Hillside contemporaries, A.R.T. Pontifex: 'I may be the sole survivor of the audience who saw Sir John play his first Shakespearean part, that of Shylock, at the age of about thirteen. Some years later, when he first played the part professionally, a theatre critic wrote that this was the first time he had done so. I was about to write to correct him, when Sir John's mother beat me to it, enclosing a photo of her son equipped with a black beard and a knife. I was about three years junior to him. I can remember him "shooing" me away from some gathering of senior boys – in his eyes I was a nasty little "new-bug".'

When not keeping the juniors in their place or starring in the works of Lewis Carroll and William Shakespeare, the boy Gielgud was engrossed in Ellen Terry's memoirs and the *Daily Sketch* reports of the theatrical garden parties of the day. 'I was born into the purple of the Terry family, so it was natural, I suppose, that the theatre should have attracted me at an early age. It appealed to my eyes first, soon it caught at my heart, and lastly its magic reached my ear. Colour, romance, and passion – suspense, action, splendour and emotional self-indulgence – all these I longed for and revelled in from my youngest days of theatre-going.'

As a boy at Hillside John certainly didn't know that he wanted to become an actor, but he knew he loved the theatre. If he had any particular ambition as a child it was possibly to follow in the footsteps of his cousin Gordon Craig (the son of Ellen Terry and the architect and artist Edward Godwin†) and become a theatrical designer. But John's parents had more straightforward ambitions for their son. Lewis was at Eton

---

† Ellen Terry chose the surname Craig for her two illegitimate children, Edith and Gordon, when she was on holiday in Scotland and was shown a rock off the Ayrshire coast, Ailsa Craig.

and John would have followed him there had he won the necessary scholarship. Val was at Rugby, but John did not get a scholarship there either. Instead he went to Westminster, where he didn't shine, but was happy enough and resolutely maintained his enthusiasm for all things theatrical.

The first play John was taken to was J.M. Barrie's *Peter Pan*, when he was seven. A year or so later he went to see his first Shakespeare, *As You like It*, at the Coronet Theatre, Notting Hill Gate, starring the great actor-manager Sir Frank Benson. (Benson is unique among theatrical knights: the only one to be dubbed in a theatre in full costume. Sir John used to enjoy telling the story: 'It was 1916 and there was a special performance at Drury Lane to mark the three hundredth anniversary of Shakespeare's death. Benson was playing Caesar and during the interval, after the murder scene, King George V summoned him to the Royal Box. There was no sword, so someone rushed round to Simmonds, the theatrical costumiers in King Street, Covent Garden, to borrow one. The King then knighted Benson and great cheers rose from the huge company behind the curtain. Sir George Alexander then went out front to explain to the mystified audience what had happened, and of course the audience went mad too.')

As a teenager in London in the teens of the century, John would go to the theatre as often as he was able and later to the music hall to see 'the greats'. He saw Adeline Genée dance and heard Marie Lloyd and Vesta Tilley sing. He saw Sarah Bernhardt and Eleonora Duse and, of course, his great-aunt Ellen Terry. 'I fell madly in love with Ellen the first time I saw her on the stage. What I remember most about her is her movement, although she was then in her seventies, deaf, rather blind and very vague. But when she came on you really believed she was walking on the flagstones of Venice or in the fields of Windsor. She moved with an extraordinary spontaneity and grace, holding her skirts gathered in two hands or bunched up over one arm, and crossed the stage with an unforgettable impression of swiftness.'

When John wasn't at the theatre or reading about the theatre he was enjoying his own amateur theatricals. All the young Gielguds – the three boys and their younger sister Eleanor – were enthusiastic actors, but John was the most devoted to the cause. Of these early amateur productions the one he remembered best marked his debut as Orlando in *As You Like It*. He was sixteen and joined a group of friends to perform the play in the open air in a rectory garden at St Leonards-on-Sea. By his own admission, he was a somewhat vain young man. 'I affected very light grey flannels braced much too high, silk socks, broad-brimmed black soft hats, and even, I blush to admit, an eye-glass upon occasion, and I wore my hair very long and washed it a great deal to make it look fluffy and romantic. For Orlando, I slipped off to a hairdresser in St Leonards and asked the man to wave it – "For a play", I added hastily. "Certainly, sir," he said. "I suppose you'd be in the Pierrot Company that's opening on the Pier this week." Undaunted, I strode on to the lawn at the first performance, drew my sword fiercely, and declaimed, "Forbear, and eat no more!", but unfortunately I tripped over a large log and fell flat on my face. This was only the beginning of my troubles, for in the last act, when I pointed to the path where I was expecting Rosalind, with "Ah, here comes Ganymede", no Ganymede was to be seen. I said the line again, with a little less confidence this time; still no one appeared. I looked helplessly round, to find the prompter, his hands to his mouth, whispering as loudly as he dared across the hundred yards that separated us, "She's changed back into her girl's clothes a scene too soon!"'

It was at about the time of this inauspicious Orlando that John told his parents of his desire to go onto the stage. They had hoped that he might try for an Oxford scholarship, but having extracted an undertaking from him that should he not have had some measure of success as an actor by the age of twenty-five he would give it up and train to become an architect, reluctantly they allowed their stage-struck son to leave Westminster and enter for a scholarship at Lady Benson's dramatic school in the Cromwell Road, London. This scholarship he won. His parents may not have been overjoyed, but his Terry grandmother was delighted:

Dear Old Jack,

I am delighted to hear of your intended real start in a profession you love, and wish you every success. You must not anticipate a bed of roses, for on the stage as in every other profession there are 'rubs and arrows' to contend with. 'Be kind and affable to all your co-mates, but if possible be intimate with none of them.' This is a quotation of my parents' advice to me and I pass it on as I have proved it to be very sound. Theatrical intimacy breeds jealousy of a petty kind which is very disturbing. I hope you may have many chances with your various studies and prove yourself worthy.

I am returning on Monday and shall, I hope, have an opportunity to have a good old talk with you.

Meanwhile, my love and congratulations,
Your affectionate grandmother,
Kate Lewis

It was in the summer of 1921, when John was just seventeen, that he won his scholarship to Constance Benson's little academy. There were, in all, no more than thirty students and of these only four were men. 'This, of course, led to great competition amongst us, so Lady Benson used to split up the good parts (such as Hamlet or Sir Peter Teazle), so that none of us should be made to feel important or indispensable, and made each of us play the same part in different scenes. When there were too many male characters in a play, the slim girls played the young men's parts, and the fat ones would appear in "character". I loved the rehearsal classes, but was less keen on the fencing, dancing and elocution which completed the curriculum. There was also a "gesture" class once a week, which Lady Benson took herself. One of her exercises was to make us rush in and express different emotions with the same line of dialogue. It must have been distinctly comic to see twenty-five young women and four self-conscious young men rushing through a door one after the other, uttering with hate, fear, disgust or joy the remark "Baby's burning".'

It was while he was at Lady Benson's, where, by his own account, he was regarded as 'a talented but conceited pupil', that John Gielgud made his first appearance at the Old Vic. Having heard that drama students were sometimes engaged as unpaid walk-ons there, he made his way to the celebrated theatre in the Waterloo Road and, at the age of seventeen, found himself cast as the Herald in Robert Atkins' production of *Henry V*. John only had one line – 'Here is the number of the slaughter'd French' – and no mention in the programme, but it was a start.

Henry V was in November 1921. In the following spring Gielgud had three more walk-on parts at the Vic, in *Peer*

Gynt, in *King Lear* and in a play by Halcott Glover about Wat
Tyler. These weren't speaking roles, but they did earn John a
mention in the programme where he was listed as 'Mr
Giulgud'. Sixty years later, talking to Sir John about those
early 'walk-ons' at the Vic, the production he remembered
best was *Peer Gynt* with Russell Thorndike, Sybil Thorndike's
younger brother, in the title role. Sir John still had his copy
of the programme (price 2*d*), on the front of which he had
noted at the time: 'A wonderful play – almost realized.
Russell Thorndike is remarkably fine and clever. I am very
glad to have taken part in it.'

When his year at Lady Benson's was up, nepotism secured
him his first proper job. His second cousin, Phyllis Neilson-
Terry, offered him £4 a week to play a few lines, understudy
and be an assistant stage manager in a touring production
of a play by J.B. Fagan called *The Wheel*. The tour opened
in Bradford – to the incurably theatrical young Gielgud a
wonderfully romantic city because Henry Irving had died
there – and took in the usual range of not-altogether
glamorous dates in the North and the Midlands. During
their week in Oxford, one of the other members of the
company, Alexander Sarner, with whom he was sharing
lodgings (in the charmingly named Paradise Square),
suggested to John that one year at drama school wasn't
enough: John was only eighteen and if he could get any
more training he should.

John took Sarner's advice to heart and, when the tour was
over, he presented himself at the Royal Academy of Dramatic
Art in Gower Street and managed to win himself another
scholarship. He did well at RADA, where his contemporaries
included Robert Harris, Beatrix Lehmann, Veronica Turleigh,

Mervyn Johns and George Howe, who was to become a close friend and colleague over the years. If Sybil Thorndike,[†] one of the visiting teachers at RADA, is to be believed, John stood out from the crowd: 'One class I had, it must have been about 1922, was really awful – they were all like a lot of governesses, no power, and I said, "You're all terrible, no fire, no guts, you've none of you got anything in you except that boy over there, the tall one, what's your name?" And he said, "It's John Gielgud," and I said, "Well, you're the only one." The rest of them had no voices, and I was furious with the principal because all his pupils were perfect ladies and gentlemen and that's no way to do Greek tragedy. They all looked as though they were training to be Gerald du Maurier.'

By the end of his first term at RADA, John had secured his second proper professional engagement. His mother happened to know Nigel Playfair (barrister turned actor-manager), who came to see John in the end-of-term production of Barrie's *The Admirable Crichton* and immediately offered him a small part in a new play he was presenting at the Regent Theatre, opposite St Pancras Station. The role was that of Felix, the Poet Butterfly, in *The Insect Play* by the Czech brothers Karel and Josef Capek, a somewhat 'modern' piece that viewed humanity in terms of insects. The cast also included Angela Baddeley, Elsa Lanchester and John's favourite teacher from RADA, Claude Rains, but the play was a flop and John felt ineffective and even embarrassed in his part. 'I wore white flannels, pumps,

---

† Then forty, and a well-established classical star. She created Shaw's Saint Joan two years later and became a Dame in 1931.

a silk shirt, a green laurel-wreath, fair hair, and a golden battledore and shuttlecock . . . I am surprised the audience did not throw things at me.'†

Nigel Playfair's next venture at the Regent Theatre was more successful. It was *Robert E. Lee* by the poet John Drinkwater, directed by Playfair and the author, and featuring most of the company from *The Insect Play*. John, understudying Claude Rains and playing the small part of an orderly, was relieved and grateful to be retained, the more so because, while appearing in the play in the evening, he was able to complete his studies at RADA during the day.

At the end of 1923, his RADA training behind him, the nineteen-year-old Gielgud managed to get himself cast as Charley in a Christmas revival of Brandon Thomas's classic farce *Charley's Aunt*, which played twice daily at the Comedy Theatre for six weeks. It was directed by Amy Brandon-Thomas, daughter of the author, 'who arrived in a large grey squirrel coat and strode onto the stage bristling with authority'. John did not feel his director gave him the scope he would have liked. 'She very soon informed me that the play was a classic – every move, nay, every garment worn by the actors was sacrosanct, and no deviation of any kind was to be tolerated for a moment.'

It was during the run of *Charley's Aunt* that John first succumbed to the sin of 'corpsing', giggling in performance.

---

† Sir John gave me an original photograph of himself in the role: 'I am happy to get rid of it.' He felt the photograph was 'so revolting' he would not allow it to appear when his first volume of memoirs, *Early Stages*, was published in 1939. Later, his view of the picture was mellower, more amused, which is why you will find it reproduced between pages 52 and 53.

'Miss Brandon-Thomas would descend on us again and lecture us severely. Laughing on the stage is a disgraceful habit and she was perfectly right to make a fuss about it. . . . My most disgraceful exhibition occurred years afterwards in *The Importance of Being Earnest*, when, at a very hot matinee, rather poorly attended, I suddenly noticed four old ladies, in different parts of the stalls, not only fast asleep, but hanging down over the edges of their seats like discarded marionettes.' John Worthing and Algernon Moncrieff were rapidly reduced to hysteria. 'The muffins we were eating refused to go down our throats, and by the end of the scene the audience were roaring with laughter, not at the play, but at our hopeless efforts to keep ourselves under control.' John's verdict on his Christmas outing in *Charley's Aunt* was that it was a useful experience, physically exhausting if not intellectually demanding. Even more useful, and certainly much more taxing, was his next engagement.

In 1923, J.B. Fagan, an Ulsterman and actor turned playwright and producer, founded the Oxford Playhouse in a disused big game museum on the city's Woodstock Road, and invited John to join the company. 'I have no idea how my new employers heard of me or why they should have thought me likely to be promising material.' Fagan wanted to establish a serious repertory theatre in Oxford and launched his venture with an ambitious first season and a remarkable team of young actors that included Flora Robson, Tyrone Guthrie, Raymond Massey and Richard Goolden. Between January 1924 and August 1925 Gielgud appeared in a total of eighteen different productions at the Oxford Playhouse. He played a wide variety of roles in works by Goldsmith and Congreve, by Bernard Shaw and J.M. Synge, A.A. Milne and Somerset Maugham, by Chekhov and Ibsen, Maeterlinck and Pirandello. 'The biggest success of the first season was *Love for Love* which shocked North Oxford and a lot of our regular patrons, but delighted a large section of the University, and drew many people to the Playhouse for the first time, chiefly I am afraid, on account of its scandalous dialogue and improper situations.' Clearly, it was a different world. 'It was an ambitious programme, but great fun. I lived in Oxford in a tiny flat in the High and earned £8 a week, a marvellous sum to me in those days.'†

Surprisingly, Fagan did not offer Gielgud any Shakespeare, but in 1924, not in Oxford but in London, John did manage to appear in *Romeo and Juliet* – twice. In February he played Paris and understudied the Romeo of Gyles Isham – Oxford University's golden boy in the early 1920s‡ – in an amateur production staged at the RADA theatre. Then, in April, John received a most unusual letter:

† In 1973, to mark the golden jubilee of the Oxford Playhouse, I was invited to stage a celebratory evening at the theatre, now located in Beaumont Street, Oxford. The company was led by three of the original members: Dame Flora Robson, Richard Goolden and Sir John, who recited a favourite speech from *Richard II*. For the first time I saw the famous 'Terry tears' at close range. At the rehearsal and in performance, at exactly the same moment, tears simply tumbled down Sir John's face.

‡ And, for what it's worth, the reason why the present author's first name is also spelt with a 'y'. My father was an undergraduate at Oxford in the late 1920s and an admirer of Gyles Isham, who had been President of the Union and Editor of *Isis* as well as President of OUDS. As a professional actor he did not fulfil his early promise, and he gave up his stage and screen career at the outbreak of the Second World War. He succeeded to the family baronetcy in 1941 and failed to become MP for Kettering in 1950.

2nd April 1924

Dear Mr Gielgud,

If you would like to play the finest lead among the plays by the late William Shakespeare, will you please call upon Mr Peacock and Mr Ayliff at the Regent Theatre on Friday at 2.30 pm. Here is an opportunity to become a London Star in a night.

Please confirm.

Yours very truly,
Akerman May

It transpired that Barry Jackson was planning to put on *Romeo and Juliet* at the Regent Theatre, to be directed by H.K. Ayliff, with Gwen Ffrangcon-Davies (then twenty-eight and Jackson's leading lady at the Birmingham Repertory Theatre) as Juliet, and they wanted John for Romeo. Gielgud leapt at the opportunity, naturally yearning for a triumph, but actually achieving what he later described as 'a pretty good disaster': 'I had the most terrible clothes, to begin with, and the most wickedly unbecoming wig . . . I didn't know how to move. I think I spoke not badly; but we had a very, very drastic director; and I just wasn't ready. I didn't know how to select what I wanted to do, or put over emotion. I just enjoyed indulging in my own emotions, and imagined that that was acting. I only learnt, long afterwards, that you may indulge your emotions in imagining a part, but you mustn't allow them free rein until you have selected exactly what you want to show the audience, and how much you should show while you're doing it.'

Ayliff was a hard task-master and not easily satisfied. The cast was forced to play the dress rehearsal with the safety curtain down because Jackson had invited an audience and Ayliff thought the play wasn't ready for one. When it did open, the critical reception was mixed for the company in general and poor for Gielgud in particular: 'unduly consumptive', 'niminy piminy', 'scant of virility'. Ivor Brown pronounced: 'Mr Gielgud has the most meaningless legs imaginable.' Indeed Gielgud had been painfully aware of his awkward gait and mannered posturing ever since Lady Benson had told him he walked like 'a cat with rickets'. It took him years to gain full command over his physical movements and appearance on stage: 'As a young actor I pranced and was very self-conscious. Then I became too graceful and posed. Now that I am less shy and able to study myself with more detachment, I have tried to control my physical mannerisms by observing them and asking to have them checked by others, which I was originally too vain and shy to do.'

Romeo and Juliet did at least afford Gielgud his one and only experience of music hall. 'Gwen and I were engaged, at rather a large salary as I recall, to do the balcony scene at the London Coliseum. We were given a terrible set, with a pink cardboard balcony and we followed a huge man called Teddy Brown, who weighed twenty stone and played the xylophone. The Houston Sisters came on after us and one of them did a sort of imitation of me with a Scottish accent and "A thousand times goodnight" and brought the house down.'

After the disappointment of *Romeo* in London, Gielgud was glad to get back to Oxford where, on the whole, his work was being rather better received and where, happily, he achieved his first notable success, as Trofimov in *The Cherry Orchard*. 'It was the first time I ever went on stage and felt that perhaps I could really act.' Chekhov was still a relatively unknown quantity as far as British audiences were concerned and J.B. Fagan's production caused quite a stir. Nigel Playfair came to Oxford, admired it and invited Fagan to bring it to London, where it played first at Playfair's theatre, the Lyric, Hammersmith, and then moved on to the Royalty. In London the play was given a wildly mixed reception. Some critics were vituperative. A few were bewildered. Most were enthusiastic. One or two were ecstatic. In the *Sunday Times* James Agate, doyen of British drama critics of the period, was unequivocal: 'I suggest that *The Cherry Orchard* is one of the great plays of the world.' He was equally generous about Gielgud's performance as Trofimov: 'perfection itself', he called it.

The overall success of *The Cherry Orchard* inspired Philip Ridgeway, a northern impresario and a comparative newcomer to London, to attempt to mount a complete 'Chekhov Season' with productions of *The Seagull*, *The Three Sisters*, *Ivanov* and *Uncle Vanya*, and he invited John to join the company. *The Seagull* was directed by A.E. Filmer. Gielgud played Konstantin, 'a very romantic character, a sort of miniature Hamlet', and received favourable notices from the press, but severe criticism from several of his friends who found his movements mannered and his diction affected. The play was a success at the Little Theatre in 1925, but when, four years later, it was revived briefly at the Arts, Gielgud was disappointed in both the production and his performance. He was anxious to make changes, but A.E. Filmer wanted to leave well alone: 'What a pity you always want to gild the lily.'

Philip Ridgeway followed up *The Seagull* with his second Chekhov, *The Three Sisters*, presented at a tiny theatre he was leasing out at Barnes. For this production he had engaged the legendary Russian director and disciple of Stanislavsky, Theodore Komisarjevsky, known to friends and colleagues as 'Komis'. Despite the fact that Komis deliberately distorted the nature of Tusenbach, making him handsome rather than plain, and forced John to play against the grain of the part, the production was well received. But its success notwithstanding, the rest of the Chekhov season didn't materialise. Komis did direct one more Russian play for Philip Ridgeway and John played in it, but it wasn't *Ivanov*. It was *Katerina* by Andreyev in which John played a betrayed middle-aged husband, 'a sort of Slavonic Othello', and felt he cut quite a dash. James Agate agreed – with reservations. 'Mr Gielgud is becoming one of our most admirable actors: there is mind behind everything he does. Only he must avoid the snag of portentousness, of being intense about nothing in particular.'

Komis was an eccentric and not always comfortable director, but over the next ten years Gielgud worked with him in four more productions and found him both stimulating and helpful. In 1963, when Sir John came to write *Stage Directions*, his book about the art and craft of the theatre, he acknowledged his debt to Komis for 'teaching me not to act from outside, seizing on obvious effects and histrionics; to avoid the temptations of showing off; to work from within to present a character, and to absorb the atmosphere and general background of a play . . . He also gave me my first important lesson in trying to act with relaxation – the secret of all good acting.'

In 1925, after *The Cherry Orchard* had finished its run at the Oxford Playhouse in January and before it opened in May at the Lyric, Hammersmith, Gielgud got the chance to understudy Noel Coward in his controversial drama *The Vortex*. The opportunity came his way thanks, in part, to his ability to play the piano – a gift he claimed to have inherited from his father. 'I went to see Noel at the Royalty Theatre in Dean Street, very apprehensive, of course, but very thrilled to meet him. His dressing room was full of bottles of Chanel No. 5, with twenty dressing gowns in the wardrobe.' Gielgud understudied Coward in *The Vortex* at the Royalty, the Comedy and the Little Theatre, and actually went on for him on three nerve-wracking occasions before taking over the part for the final four weeks of the run. 'I was very much aware that Noel was an infinitely better Nicky Lancaster than I was. It was a highly-strung, nervous, hysterical part which depended a lot upon emotion.'

A year later Gielgud again took over from Coward and played Lewis Dodd in the stage version of Margaret Kennedy's romantic best-seller *The Constant Nymph*. It was his first leading role in a West End hit and his first taste of a long run: 'I found it terribly irksome. The part was extremely tiring, and I had a bad time because the company didn't like me very much. They resented Noel leaving and I wasn't very happy with the direction that I got, such as it was. But the play was an enormous success and I learned the hard way, how to carry this very long and exhausting part for more than a year and afterwards for quite a long tour.'

While he was appearing in *The Constant Nymph* young Gielgud did as he had done since he began his career as a professional actor and appeared regularly in one-off Sunday performances and special matinees of a wide variety of other plays. At the Savoy, for example, he appeared as Ferdinand in a few performances of *The Tempest*. At the Apollo he played Cassio in a special performance of *Othello*. At Wyndham's he appeared with Mrs Patrick Campbell in *Ghosts* for a series of special matinees marking the centenary of Ibsen's birth in 1828. 'Hardly anybody came. Mrs Campbell was very cross, especially that none of her Society friends bothered to turn up. She dearly loved a lord. She would say to me, out loud, in the middle of a scene, "The Marquis and Marchioness of So-and-so are in front again."'

When the tour of *The Constant Nymph* was over, Gielgud set off for New York and his Broadway debut as the Tsarevitch Alexander in Alfred Neumann's *The Patriot*. The play was a flop and John had hardly disembarked from the SS *Berlin*, which had taken him to New York, before he was setting sail for London again. During the next eighteen months he appeared in ten different plays in London. None was a notable success. 'They were terrible plays, but I took everything that was offered to me, pretty well. I was the leading man, which was a new experience for me; I was getting good billing and a good salary; so I thought that perhaps acting was just being in work and doing whatever came along.'

John Gielgud was now twenty-five and a busy working actor with a bit of a name and something of a reputation. He didn't have to throw in his hand and become an architect.

three

'I'M A STAR!'
1929–1933

'As a beginner my career was uneven and seemed to lead in no particularly definite direction. I was tall, mannered, highly strung. I spoke and moved jerkily, my emotions were sincere but undisciplined, I had some gift for character, some feeling for poetry, some idea of timing in comedy, yet my sense of humour was strictly limited by a youthful self-importance and terror of being ridiculed. I longed for encouragement and popularity.'

In 1973, when Sir John returned to the Oxford Playhouse to mark the theatre's golden jubilee, I asked him who had most influenced him at the outset of his career. 'J.B. Fagan here in Oxford, Nigel Playfair, Barry Jackson and Komisarjevsky were the first to show an interest in my early amateurish efforts at self-expression. They developed my taste by engaging me to act in fine plays with many gifted players. I was observant and industrious, though also vain and affected.

'It was a good time for experimental work, done modestly and cheaply. Classical revivals were out of fashion. The actor-managers' reign was over. The London theatres were recovering from the confusion of the 1914–18 war. Noel Coward was writing his first plays. Basil Dean's productions at the St Martin's were the most ambitious contribution to the new era. The other West End theatres were filled with light comedies, farces and melodramas, many of them, even in those far-off days, imported from America.'

When Gielgud first arrived on the scene, who were the leading players? 'The most popular stars of the period were probably Gerald du Maurier, Henry Ainley, Marie Tempest, Gladys Cooper, and Matheson Lang, with his costume and melodramas, carrying on the romantic tradition of Fred Terry and Martin Harvey, both of whom only appeared occasionally in London but still toured the provinces successfully. Ellen Terry had made her last professional appearance at the Lyric as the Nurse in Doris Keane's *Romeo and Juliet* in 1919, and Bernhardt and Duse were about to make their farewell visits to London under the banner of C.B. Cochran, who also presented the Guitrys, with Yvonne Printemps and Reinhardt's great spectacles *The Miracle* and *Sumurun* at Olympia and the Coliseum. Karsavina was still appearing with the Russian Ballet of Diaghilev at the old Alhambra.

'Players still took curtain calls after every act of a play, even if they had just acted a death scene, and understudies seemed to appear with great frequency in leading parts, especially at matinees. This was lucky for the understudies (and I have always boasted that I never understudied a leading part in my young days without getting an opportunity to play it), but it was less agreeable for the public. I well remember my baffled rage as a boy, when, after three or four hours' queueing for the pit during my holidays from school, the slip fluttering from the programme told of the absence of the star whom I most desired to see.'

By 1929 Gielgud, by his own account, had already been 'a leading man (of a sort) in the West End for three years', but was by no means a star whom any 'most desired to see'. Lilian Baylis and Harcourt Williams changed all that.

Miss Baylis, founder of the Old Vic and Sadler's Wells companies, was one of the most unlikely and influential figures in the history of the British theatre. Born in 1874 she went with her family to South Africa at the age of sixteen and embarked there on a musical career which was interrupted in 1895 when she returned to London to help her aunt, Emma Cons, run the Victoria Theatre opposite Waterloo Station as a temperance hall known as the Royal Victorian Coffee Musical Hall. When Emma Cons died in 1912, her niece Lilian took over the management and began to transform the theatre into what was to become the legendary Old Vic: a place where drama and opera of real quality could be brought to ordinary people. Between 1914 and 1923 all of Shakespeare's plays were performed at the Old Vic and when drama threatened to overwhelm opera in the theatre's programme, Lilian Baylis took over, rebuilt and, in 1931, opened the Sadler's Wells Theatre as a home for opera and ballet. Single-minded, determined, intensely religious, with the manner of a shuffling landlady rather than a purveyor of art for the masses, Miss Baylis was a formidable individual who succeeded against all the odds and managed to maintain the most remarkable artistic standards despite continuous financial hardship. Her secretary is said once to have looked into her office and found Miss Baylis on her knees and at prayer: 'Dear God, send me a good Hamlet – but make him cheap.'

In 1929 Lilian Baylis engaged Harcourt Williams as her producer† at the Old Vic. Williams was then almost fifty, an established actor who had appeared with many of the 'greats': Ellen Terry, Frank Benson, George Alexander, Martin Harvey and John Barrymore, among them. He came to the Vic with the beginnings of a reputation as an innovator that grew considerably during his five years on the Waterloo Road. He was an intellectual (at least by theatre standards), a seasoned performer, an ardent admirer of the designer Gordon Craig and a keen student of Harley Granville-Barker's *Prefaces to Shakespeare*. His productions were initially treated with suspicion, if not disdain, then gradually acclaimed as landmarks in the history of Shakespearean presentation.

When he arrived at the Vic, Harcourt Williams had no doubt that the two figures he wanted to lead the company were John Gielgud and Martita Hunt. After protracted negotiations – Miss Baylis took her usual line: 'We can't afford stars' – he secured the services of both of them and John moved south of the Thames to begin one of the most exciting and rewarding phases of his career. 'In the West End I had been earning £50 a week, a not inconsiderable sum in those days, and getting billed above the title. At the Old Vic I was offered £10 and leading parts, but none of them specified. I wasn't sure whether or not to accept. I took advice from Edith Evans. She was appearing in *The Lady with*

---

† In the theatre, until the 1950s, the person responsible for the creative and artistic direction of a play – its *mise-en-scène* – was known as the producer. The term 'director', adopted from the film industry, only began to gain currency in the theatre after the Second World War.

the Lamp and very sweetly, and most unusually, agreed to see me between her matinee and her evening performance. She said, "If you want to learn how to play Shakespeare, I think you'd be very wise to accept it." So I did.'

Gielgud stayed with the Old Vic Company for just two seasons, but in the twenty months between September 1929 and April 1931 he played the whole gamut of Shakespeare's leading men: Romeo, Richard II, Oberon, Mark Antony, Orlando, Macbeth, Hamlet, Hotspur, Prospero, Antony, Malvolio, Benedick and Lear. He also took on Antonio in *The Merchant of Venice*, Cleante in Molière's *The Imaginary Invalid*, the title role in Pirandello's *The Man With a Flower in his Mouth*, Lord Trinket in George Colman's 1761 comedy *The Jealous Wife*, and, since Harcourt Williams was an enthusiastic Shavian, the Emperor in *Androcles and the Lion* and Sergius in *Arms and the Man*.

John's first performance was as Romeo. Adele Dixon played Juliet, Martita Hunt the Nurse, Gyles Isham was Mercutio and the company included Donald Wolfit as Tybalt. The production was not a success, as Wolfit later recollected: 'Almost everyone was blamed for taking the play at such a speed that the verse and poetry were entirely lost. The Prologue does indeed speak of "the two hours' traffic of our stage" and we nearly achieved that.' Even Harcourt Williams, who encouraged the playing of the verse with speed and verve, was disappointed with Gielgud's Romeo. 'The least interesting performance of his two years at the Old Vic,' he called it. 'He certainly gave little hint of the power to come, albeit it was a thoughtful, well-graced performance, and he spoke beautifully. But he never touched the last scenes. He failed to bring off the distracted boy jolted by disaster into full manhood; the ecstasy, too, of the last moments transcending death escaped him.'

Gielgud didn't achieve particular success at the Vic that season until the fourth production, but the triumph when it came was a notable one. Ever since seeing Ernest Milton's memorable Richard II in the 1920/21 Vic Season, Gielgud had wanted to play the part and now, in November 1929, and wearing Ernest Milton's old costume, he seized his chance. Kitty Black, who came to know Gielgud well years later when she was a secretary in the office of 'Binkie' Beaumont at H.M. Tennent, saw the production. She was fifteen and went with a party of girls from Roedean: 'Our class was "doing" the play for School Certificate. At first sight I had hated the pale effeminate boy he appeared to be, but by the end of the second scene I had fallen in love with the magical voice and as the play ended I was sobbing uncontrollably. Merely by describing his performance throughout the exam I sailed through with an A+.'

The critics too gave Gielgud's performance full marks and several suggested, immediately and later, that his interpretation of the role was the spearhead of a new kind of acting. Talking about it in retrospect, Gielgud disagreed: 'I think it was more the result of an old kind of acting that I inherited from the Terrys and what I call the *panache* actors I admired so much in my youth: a certain gift of projection and an unreal kind of romantic acting, which I did with so much conviction for myself that I did manage to convince the audience. Richard is, after all, a very affected and elaborately romantic, attitudinising, part. But now, when I listen to my old recordings, they sound to me very voice-conscious, and I'm rather ashamed to think that I was so contented with that kind of acting. I don't really believe it has the truth in it that I would like, except, of course, that in *Richard II* the man is meant to be studying himself and indulging in his own sorrows, so that it may have been more appropriate.'

At the time, Gielgud's Richard II was considered to have truth and beauty. The *Observer* critic Ivor Brown called it 'exquisite'. Gielgud's producer, Harcourt Williams, saw it as the turning-point in the season: 'His playing of the abdication scene will live in my mind as one of the great things I have witnessed in the theatre. A tall, willowy figure in black velvet, surmounted by a fair head, the pale agonised face set beneath a glittering crown.'

In the spring of 1930, when Gielgud had not yet turned twenty-six, Harcourt Williams suggested to him that he might like to try a real Shakespearean heavyweight and have a go at Macbeth. Given Gielgud's age and physical appearance at the time, it was unlikely casting, but now he was taking Shakespeare at the flood and rose unhesitatingly to the challenge. He based the look and feel of his performance on what he had read and heard of Henry Irving in the role: 'My physical picture of Macbeth was derived principally from the drawings of Irving by Bernard Partridge which I had seen in a souvenir of the Lyceum production. I made up in the last act with whitened hair and bloodshot eyes, trying to resemble as nearly as I could "the gaunt, famished wolf" of Ellen Terry's description of Irving.'

Gielgud achieved surprising success in the part, helped no doubt by a fine Lady Macbeth from Martita Hunt who was herself only thirty. The rest of the company, the public and the critics were equally impressed. James Agate declared: 'For the first time in my experience Macbeth retained his hold upon the play until the end.' Indeed, Agate had been so convinced that Gielgud would not be able to sustain the performance that he had gone round to congratulate him during the interval. In the event, Agate was bowled over by Gielgud's sustained achievement: 'in the old phrase, the actor carried us away.' Ivor Brown was just as enthusiastic. He exhorted his readers: 'See *Macbeth* at the Old Vic and be able to tell your children that you saw the great John Gielgud in his prime.'

The next peak John was set to assault in that awe-inspiring season was *Hamlet*. When he had first met Lilian Baylis and discussed the parts he might play at the Vic, she had teased him about the possiblity of Hamlet, suggesting that there were several young players in the company who might be equally fitted to take it on – Gyles Isham being one. In the event Isham played Horatio and Gielgud played Hamlet, with Adele Dixon as Ophelia, Martita Hunt as Gertrude and Donald Wolfit as Claudius. Tyrone Guthrie described it as 'a very youthful, thrilling Hamlet' and, although Gielgud was to play the part off and on for another fourteen years, he quickly recognised the advantage of playing it young. 'Hamlet had never been allowed to be given to a very young actor until I played it. . . . I don't think anybody (except Master Betty[†]) had ever played it under thirty-five, and it made people realise the tragedy of the beginning of the play in a way that an older man can never achieve.'

---

† William Betty, 1791–1874, was a celebrated boy actor, who made his debut aged eleven. He quit the stage in 1808, went to Cambridge, returned to the theatre in 1812 and finally retired, aged thirty-three, in 1824.

The production – including two performances of the complete text, generally known to the cast as 'the Eternity Version' – provided a fitting climax to the season and was so successful that it secured for Miss Baylis her first West End transfer. In June the play opened at the Queen's Theatre in Shaftesbury Avenue and Gielgud received the best notices of his career: 'a great performance', 'a unique achievement', 'puts him beyond the range of arriving actors; he is in the first rank'. While Gielgud was modest about his achievement – 'I threw myself into the part like a man learning to swim and I found the text would hold me up if I sought the truth in it' – James Agate in the *Sunday Times* ran through a veritable thesaurus of superlatives: 'This actor is young, thoughtful, clever, sensitive; his performance is subtle, brilliant, vigorous, imaginative, tender and full of the right kind of ironic humour . . . I have no hesitation in saying that it is the high water mark of English Shakespearean acting in our time.'

Agate was not nearly so enthusiastic about Gielgud's next venture. Between the end of the *Hamlet* run at the Queen's and the start of the new Vic season in September, John made the first of his five appearances as John Worthing in *The Importance of Being Earnest*. This was under Sir Nigel Playfair's management at the Lyric, Hammersmith, and featured John's distinguished aunt, Mabel Terry-Lewis, as a powerful Lady Bracknell. 'She played the part beautifully, but she had no idea why it was funny at all. She said, "Why are they laughing? This line isn't funny to me."' The production was dressed and designed entirely in black and white, in the manner of Aubrey Beardsley drawings. The public, and most of the critics, enjoyed it and Gielgud revelled in a part so very different from Hamlet yet one which, in the coming years, he was to make equally his own.

At the beginning of the new season at the Old Vic, for which Miss Baylis paid him £20 a week ('I was much impressed, knowing what an agony it was for her to increase a salary'), Ralph Richardson joined the company. He was a couple of years older than John and initially the two actors were wary of one another. 'He thought that I was affected and conceited and wore unsuitably dandy clothes.' When Sir Ralph died in the autumn of 1983 Gielgud recalled their first encounter: 'When we first acted together at the Old Vic in 1930, I little thought that we might be friends. At first we were inclined to circle round each other like suspicious dogs. In our opening production I played Hotspur to his Prince Hal, and was relieved, though somewhat surprised, to discover that he was as reluctant as I to engage in the swordplay demanded in the later under-rehearsed scenes at Shrewsbury. On the first night I was amazed at his whispered instructions – surely, I thought, the audience must hear them too – "Now you hit me, cocky. Now I hit you."

'A few weeks later, as we moved into rehearsals for *The Tempest* I rather hesitatingly ventured to suggest to him a private session for examining one of our scenes together, and he immediately agreed with the greatest modesty and good humour. This was, as he has often said himself, the beginning of a friendship that was to last for fifty years.'

As well as Prince Hal and Caliban, Richardson had a particular success that season with Sir Toby Belch (to Gielgud's Malvolio) in *Twelfth Night* and Bluntschi in *Arms and the Man* (to Gielgud's Sergius). From Gielgud's viewpoint, the highspots in the 1930/31 Old Vic season were a well-regarded Prospero in *The Tempest* (at his friend Komisar-jevsky's suggestion he didn't wear a beard for the part and dressed himself up to look like Dante), a solid Antony in *Antony and Cleopatra* and an entertaining and effective Benedick in *Much Ado About Nothing*. At the end of the season he was given the option of reviving his triumphant *Hamlet* or essaying *King Lear*. Characteristically he chose the new challenge and gave a performance that was by no means universally acclaimed, but was generally recognised as showing the makings of a future Lear of greatness. 'It was distinctly ambitious of me to dare, at the age of twenty-six, to try to assume "the large effects that troop with majesty" as eighty-year-old King Lear.'

Gielgud's second season at the Old Vic may have lacked the epoch-making triumphs that characterised the first, but it broadened his range, sharpened his technique and helped further establish his already impressive reputation. That year Harold Nicolson wrote in his diary, 'I think he may well be the finest actor we have had since Irving.' Most of his contemporaries would have concurred. Gielgud himself found the experience of playing so many major roles in such a limited space of time both exhausting and exhilarating. Being thrown in at the deep end, he was forced to react instinctively to the parts, not studying the details, but imagining the whole. Many years later he recalled: 'This happened to me with all the great parts I played when I was at the Vic as a young man – Lear, Macbeth, Antony, Hamlet. In some cases, particularly in *Macbeth*, I had more success the first time than when I came to study the part more thoroughly twelve years later. I simply imagined it and acted it for the main development and broad lines of the character, without worrying about the technical, intellectual, and psychological difficulties. I played it from scene to scene as it seemed to come to me as we rehearsed the play. With only three weeks, of course, there was not time to do much more than that. I think one should dare to fly high when one is young; one may sometimes surprise oneself. It is wonderful to be able to give the imagination full play, hardly realising what an exciting danger is involved.'

After two seasons at the Old Vic, Gielgud was ready to get back to the West End and he returned to the commercial theatre in Edward Knoblock's stage version of J.B. Priestley's novel *The Good Companions*. The part of Inigo Jollifant 'made very few demands' (he rehearsed it while he was still playing King Lear at the Vic), but it was a considerable popular success and gave Gielgud his longest run since *The Constant Nymph*. He was now a fully-fledged London star, with billing and salary to match. *The Good Companions* was followed by another long West End run in *Musical Chairs* by Ronald Mackenzie. Originally entitled *The Discontents*, the play had heavy Chekhovian overtones and Gielgud felt Komisarjevsky would be the right director. The production was not without its traumas – Komis was often not in attendance: according to Gielgud, 'he had a very emotional love-life and was prone to "Russian moods"' – but when it opened it found general favour with critics and public alike and ran comfortably from April Fool's Day to New Year's Eve.

In 1932 Gielgud also made his debut as a director, producing the Oxford University Dramatic Society in *Romeo and Juliet* and persuading two notable professional actresses to lead the company of undergraduate amateurs. Peggy Ashcroft, then twenty-five, was Juliet and Edith Evans, then forty-four, the Nurse. It was the first time Peggy Ashcroft worked with Gielgud: 'The whole experience was exciting and unforgettable and it was a prologue to what was to happen to many of us under John's inspiration and leadership in the late thirties. His energetic, fresh and dancing imagination was evident from the first rehearsal: his conception of the essential youthfulness of the play, which fitted his undergraduate cast, was something that inspired us all – amateur and professional; it had a marvellous zest and speed – an impulsiveness justifying the fiery quarrels of the Montagues and the Capulets and the romantic follies of Romeo.'

Gielgud had long wanted to try his hand as a director and once he got the taste for the craft, he never lost it. Over the next two years he directed five West End shows – *Strange Orchestra* by Rodney Ackland at the St Martin's, *Sheppey* by Somerset Maugham at Wyndham's, *Spring 1600* by Emlyn Williams at the Shaftesbury, *Queen of Scots* by Gordon Daviot at the New, and Rodney Ackland's adaptation of Hugh Walpole's novel *The Old Ladies*, again at the New – as well as returning to the Old Vic to direct *The Merchant of Venice* for Harcourt Williams and going back to Oxford to direct the OUDS in *Richard II*. A few years later, in 1952, he was to claim that 'my real ambition was not to act but to direct.'

In the 1920s Gielgud had appeared in 'three or four silent films'. He did not rate his performances: 'I knew I had been perfectly ridiculous, over-acting grotesquely.' Between 1932 and 1935 he appeared in three more pictures: an unsatisfactory drama called *Insult*, a film version of *The Good Companions* (in which he couldn't really compete with the screen looks and charm of Jessie Matthews) and a frustrating (at least from Gielgud's point of view) Alfred Hitchcock thriller, *The Secret Agent*. The films brought him useful income, and exposure outside London, but his heart – and his soul – were still totally committed to the theatre. 'Since I was always acting in the theatre at night, I found filming terribly exhausting. I had to get up very early in the morning and was always fidgeting to get away by five or six for the evening performance, so I grew to dislike working for the cinema. Of course, I was paid more money than in the theatre, but I had a feeling no one thought I was sufficiently good-looking to be very successful.'

His next stage success, however, was a considerable one. Under the name Gordon Daviot, Elizabeth Mackintosh (who also wrote as Josephine Tey) had written a play called *Richard of Bordeaux*. She had been inspired by Gielgud's portrayal of Richard II at the Old Vic, but hers was a simpler, sweeter, more popular version of the story. John had reservations about the piece when he first read it, but having tried it out at the Arts Theatre, and having worked on the script and revised it with Gordon Daviot, he opened in it at the New Theatre in February 1933. It was an immediate and spectacular triumph. The *Daily Telegraph*'s critic, W.A. Darlington, reported that the audience gave it 'a glorious and full-throated roar such as the West End seldom hears in these sophisticated days.'

Gielgud directed the play himself, with costumes and sets ('simple but elegant, in very pale colours, gold and buff and white') created by 'Motley', a team of three designers – Margaret and Sophie Harris and Elizabeth Montgomery – who were to work regularly and happily with Gielgud over the next decade. The company included his first Juliet, Gwen

Ffrangcon-Davies (said Agate, if she 'is not the best actress in England there is certainly none better'), his old friend George Howe, the not-so-friendly Donald Wolfit (they never liked one another), and the young Anthony Quayle. 'Of the *Richard* rehearsals,' recalled Quayle, 'I remember how struck I was by John's clothes – his suede shoes, his beautifully cut suits, his immaculate shirts, the long gold key chain that went around his waist before diving into his trouser pocket; I had never seen the like. I remember how courteous he was to the older and very distinguished members of his cast – and well he may have been: though God-like to me in his eminence, he was only twenty-eight.'

He was only twenty-eight, but he was at the summit – and loving it. 'I had the greatest "fan" success of my whole career. Crowds mobbed me at the stage door and often followed me home to my flat nearby, ringing me up, clattering my letter-box and sending me presents.' Emlyn Williams called on Gielgud during the run of *Richard of Bordeaux*. '"I must remember to order three hundred more postcards," said John. "After the show I sit signing them in my costume as people come round. Yes, I know it's vulgar, but I can't resist it. I'm a star!"'

—— **four** ——

'THE WORLD'S BEST HAMLET'
1933-1946

John Gielgud loved *Richard of Bordeaux*, both the experience of playing it and the play itself. 'The lightness of
the style, the economy of dialogue, the ageing and
development of the character of Richard from scene to
scene, and, above all, the humour of the part, made it
infinitely easier, more attractive and more rewarding to the
actor than Shakespeare's Richard, who carries such a load of
exquisite – but utterly humourless – cadenzas in a stream of
unrelieved, self-pitying monotony.'

Richard of Bordeaux played to capacity at the New Theatre
in St Martin's Lane from 2 February 1933 to 24 March 1934
and then enjoyed a brief sell-out provincial tour. Concerning
the ending of the run, Harold Hobson (James Agate's
successor on the *Sunday Times* and the first theatre critic to be
given a knighthood) wrote: 'If you shut down all the power
stations in Britain, you could hardly lose more electricity than
went out when John Gielgud stopped playing in Gordon
Daviot's *Richard of Bordeaux* in 1934.'

Early in the summer of that year a friend said to Emlyn Williams, 'John's doing *The Maitlands*, the new Mackenzie piece. It's modern, of course. John says if his public don't see him soon in a pair of trousers they'll think he hasn't got any.' After *Richard of Bordeaux* Gielgud was anxious to appear in 'something entirely different'. For many *The Maitlands*, in which he played a dowdy, disillusioned schoolmaster, was altogether too different. It was Ronald Mackenzie's last play, completed shortly before he was killed in a car crash, and Komisarjevsky, who directed it, persuaded Gielgud to take on the less glamorous of the two leading parts in a deliberate attempt to get him to play against what his public might conceive as the Gielgud persona. Some of the public were disappointed – and a few expressed their disapproval from the gallery on the first night – but, on the whole, the critics were generous: Ivor Brown in the *Observer* found in Gielgud's performance 'all his poignant quality' plus 'a new masculinity of attack to suit the energy of the writing.'

Since the end of the run of *The Good Companions* in 1931 Gielgud had been under contract to Bronson Albery, the impresario and manager of the Criterion, Wyndham's and New theatres. His first venture with Albery had been in another, generally better regarded Mackenzie play, *Musical Chairs*, but now, towards the end of *The Maitlands'* four-month run, Albery suggested to Gielgud that he should appear in and direct a new production of *Hamlet* to open at the New in November 1934. The invitation to return to the part with which he had had such success at the Old Vic – but this time with longer for rehearsal, a more generous budget, and designs by the beloved Motleys – was irresistible.

Gielgud cast the twenty-five-year-old Jessica Tandy as Ophelia, with Laura Cowie as Gertrude, Frank Vosper as Claudius, George Howe as Polonius, Glen Byam Shaw as Laertes, Jack Hawkins as Horatio, Richard Ainley and Anthony Quayle as Rosencrantz and Guildenstern, and a twenty-year-old Alec Guinness as Osric.

Forty years on, in his autobiography, Guinness evoked the Gielgud rehearsal style: '"Come on from the left. No! No! The *other* left! – Oh, someone make him understand! – Why are you so stiff? Why don't you make me laugh?" The superb tenor voice, like a silver trumpet muffled in silk, kept up a rapid stream of commentary together with wildly contradictory instructions from the stalls while I fumbled with my little Temple edition of Shakespeare on the bare stage of the New Theatre (now the Albery). It took a whole morning to set a single page of text. Gielgud's directions to the actors were interrupted frequently, in full flight, by his calling out to the designers . . . "Motleys! Motleys! Would it be pretty to have it painted gold? Perhaps not. Oh, don't fidget, Frith Banbury! Alec Guinness, you are gabbling. Banbury, your spear is crooked. Now turn up stage. No, not you. You! Turn the other way. Oh, why can't you all *act*? Get someone to teach you to *act*!"'

Guinness was paid £7 a week for the run of *Hamlet* and, off and on, worked for Gielgud in seven productions over the next three years. 'I revered Gielgud as an artist and was totally glamourised by his personality, but he was a strict disciplinarian intolerant of any slovenliness of speech and exasperated by youthful tentativeness. He was a living monument of impatience. At that time he was thirty years old, at the height of his juvenile powers and, with *Richard of*

Bordeaux behind him (I saw him in the part fifteen times), commanded a huge following throughout the country. He held his emperor-like head higher than high, rather thrown back, and carried himself with ramrod straightness. He walked, or possibly tripped, with slightly bent knees to counteract a childhood tendency to flat-footedness. His arm movements were inclined to be jerky and his large bony hands a little stiff. A suggestion of fluidity in his gestures was imparted by his nearly always carrying, when on stage, a big white silk handkerchief. His resemblance to his distinguished old father was remarkable and he combined an air of patrician Polish breeding with Terry charm and modest theatricality. There was nothing he lacked, as far as I could see, except tact. His tactless remarks, over the decades, have joined the ranks of the happiest theatre legends of our time and, apart from their sheer funniness, they have always been entirely forgivable because they spring spontaneously from the heart without a glimmer of malice.

'It was after a week of rehearsing *Hamlet* that he spoke "spontaneously" to me, with shattering effect. "What's happened to you?" he cried. "I thought you were rather good. You're terrible. Oh, go away! I don't want to see you again!"

'I hung around at rehearsals until the end of the day and then approached him cautiously. "Excuse me, Mr Gielgud, but am I fired?"

'"No! Yes! No, of course not. But go away. Come back in a week. Get someone to teach you how to act. Try Martita Hunt." So I went back to Westbourne Road, sat on my narrow rickety bed and had a little weep. I didn't dare tell Martita, who had become a friend, what had happened as

I felt she would be as upset as I was and might start telephoning John. I mooched around for a week, mostly walking in London parks, and then, heart in mouth, reported back for rehearsals in St Martin's Lane. He seemed pleased to see me, heaped praise on my Osric and laughed delightedly at the personality (very water-fly) which I had assumed. I could swear I wasn't doing anything differently from what I had done before but, suddenly and briefly, I was teacher's pet. "Motleys! Motleys, you should give him a hat with a lot of feathers, like the Duchess of Devonshire!"

'We opened in November, the production was a sell-out, running for about ten months, and John's Hamlet was his definitive performance in the part. I watched most of it from the wings every single night, as did two or three others of the younger actors. At Christmas he gave me a handsome edition of Ellen Terry's letters in which he wrote, "To Alec, who grows apace", and then a quotation from Act V, which has remained my motto throughout life, "The readiness is all."'

Hamlet was a commercial triumph. The production cost just £1,000 to stage. Before it opened, on 14 November 1934, the advance bookings exceeded £1,000, a record amount for a non-musical play. The critic J.C. Trewin declared it 'the key Shakespearean revival of its period', but on the first night it was not a total critical success. Herbert Farjeon thought that the added burden of direction had destroyed some of the youthful poignancy and spontaneous originality of the first conception, Raymond Mortimer considered Gielgud's Hamlet now 'too purely the intellectual', and James Agate reckoned it was 'Everest half scaled'. But whatever the critics thought, the public was unequivocally enthusiastic and the production ran for 155 performances (to 30 March 1935 at the New Theatre, followed by a provincial tour), a record beaten previously only by Henry Irving and subsequently only by Richard Burton in Gielgud's own production in New York in 1964.

I once asked Gielgud if Hamlet was 'the ultimate role' for every actor. 'For every young actor, yes.' Why? 'Because it is the ultimate test. The part demands declamation, macabre humour, passionate violence, philosophical reflection, the combining of action and intelligence. Hamlet is the many-sided, multi-talented Elizabethan man – prince, son, courtier, swordsman, philosopher, lover, friend. All human life is there.'

Gielgud was back in period clothes and that's how he was to stay for his next ten stage appearances. The first of these, in the summer of 1935, was the title part in André Obey's *Noah*, adapted for the London production by Gielgud himself with his director, Michel Saint-Denis, who had been responsible for the original *Compagnie des Quinze* production in France in 1931. 'For me,' said Gielgud, 'Saint-Denis' influence was as important as, though very different from, that of Komis. . . . Michel came to rehearsals every day with complete notes of every movement, every piece of business, every characterisation. . . . Komisarjevsky, by contrast, never had notes but would appear to improvise, though I think he had everything very clearly in his head. He was sympathetic to an actor's struggles, mistakes and experiments, while Saint-Denis was something of a martinet, with a very orderly French mind.'

Noah suffered from a short rehearsal period (just three weeks), an uneven script (Gielgud and Saint-Denis were adapting the text as used in the New York production – it

Young Jack: John Gielgud in 1913, aged nine. (*Hulton Getty Picture Collection*)

John Gielgud, third from right, as Mark Antony in the Hillside School production of *Julius Caesar*, 1916. (*Sir John Gielgud's collection*)

The Poet Butterfly in *The Insect Play*, Regent Theatre, 1923. Not one of Gielgud's favourite roles – or photographs. 'Looking at it, I am surprised that the audience didn't throw things at me . . .' (*Author's collection*)

Romeo and Juliet, Regent Theatre, 1924, with Gwen Ffrangcon-Davies, aged twenty-eight, and Gielgud, a few weeks after his twentieth birthday. (*Mander & Mitchenson Theatre Collection*)

Gielgud's first *Hamlet*, with Donald Wolfit as Claudius, Old Vic, 1930. (*Mander & Mitchenson Theatre Collection*)

Macbeth, Old Vic, 1930. 'My physical picture of Macbeth was derived principally from the drawings of Irving by Bernard Partridge which I had seen in a souvenir of the Lyceum production.' (*Mander & Mitchenson Theatre Collection*)

The first of Gielgud's five appearances as John Worthing in *The Importance of Being Earnest*,
Lyric Theatre, Hammersmith, 1930. (*Mander & Mitchenson Theatre Collection*)

Richard of Bordeaux, New
Theatre, 1933. (*Copyright
reserved/National Portrait Gallery,
London*)

Laurence Olivier as Romeo, Edith Evans as the Nurse, John Gielgud as Mercutio, *Romeo and
Juliet*, New Theatre, 1935. (*Mander & Mitchenson Theatre Collection*)

Hamlet, with Jessica Tandy as Ophelia, New Theatre, 1935. (*Theatre Museum, Victoria & Albert Museum*)

Joseph in *The School for Scandal*, Queen's Theatre, 1937. (*Author's collection*)

included such felicities as the line, 'Hey, you floozies!') and what many regarded as an over-elaborate make-up for the star player. As the Old Testament hero, Gielgud was virtually unrecognizable. Ivor Brown described his Noah as a 'mixture of Lear, Job, Tolstoy and the Old Man of the Sea plagued with a Load of Mischief'. In general the public, however, was both charmed and intrigued by the piece ('We feel a wind blowing from somewhere very close to heaven,' said the Irish playwright Sean O'Casey) and by Gielgud's performance ('Grand acting,' O'Casey called it). The reaction from *Punch* was typical: 'It has recently been made plain that descendants are entitled to object to plays about their ancestors, and it is thought quite natural, in an age of realism on the stage, that they should object furiously to the bare idea. But none of the descendants of Noah who watched Mr John Gielgud take him out of the family frame and make him walk and talk at the New Theatre, would have dreamt of invoking privilege to stop him. For Noah is a credit to us all. Of the type of Daniel Peggotty, with moments of Mr Micawber, he is, in Mr Gielgud's hands, something much more than a delightful old boy. He is man the builder and maker – but even more, man the servant of God.'

In the autumn of 1935 John had hoped to star in a stage version of Charles Dickens' *A Tale of Two Cities*, on which he had been working with the young Terence Rattigan (who, as an Oxford undergraduate, had appeared as 'First Musician' in Gielgud's first production of *Romeo and Juliet* three years before). The project had to be abandoned, however, when Sir John Martin Harvey, who was now seventy-two and had been playing in his own adaptation of the same novel since 1899, announced that he was contemplating making another farewell tour with his own production and was concerned that the Gielgud enterprise would present unfair competition. Out of deference to the old actor-manager, Gielgud reluctantly shelved his own plan and proposed to Bronson Albery an alternative, and equally ambitious, venture: a new production of *Romeo and Juliet* with Peggy Ashcroft as Juliet, Edith Evans as the Nurse, and with Gielgud himself both directing and alternating the roles of Romeo and Mercutio with Robert Donat.

Albery bought the idea immediately, but Donat, an established stage and film star (he had just made *The Thirty-Nine Steps*, directed by Alfred Hitchcock), declined the invitation. He had plans for a production of his own that year (as, incidentally, had Ivor Novello). This he agreed to put on hold, while nonetheless preferring not to appear with Gielgud. In Donat's place Gielgud decided to cast a twenty-eight-year-old rising star, Laurence Olivier – who had also been hoping to stage his own production of the play. Gielgud and Olivier had worked together only once before, in Gielgud's production of Gordon Daviot's *Queen of Scots* the preceding year, when, at the last minute, Olivier had played Bothwell after Ralph Richardson withdrew from the part.

When *Romeo and Juliet* opened at the New Theatre in October 1935 Olivier played Romeo and Gielgud Mercutio. At the end of November they swapped roles and Gielgud stayed as Romeo for the duration of the run, which continued until the end of March, making it the longest run of the play on record. 'My scheme of alternating the parts of Romeo and Mercutio with Olivier proved very attractive to the public, and showed that it was possible to play two great parts in completely different ways without upsetting the swing and rhythm of the whole production. The only trouble came in our scenes together, when we kept on trying to speak on each other's cues.'

On the morning after the opening night, Olivier was disheartened by the tone of the reviews: 'I had always seen myself so vividly as the one and only Romeo that when the sledge-hammer of opprobrium struck its blows from every critic to a man, I was so shocked it was all I could do to get myself on to the stage for the second performance. While I was making up for this, Bronnie Albery was sweet enough to come into my room, No. 3 at the New Theatre, to attempt a few words of sympathy. I quite sincerely offered to give up the part immediately.'

In fact, those who saw both players in both roles tended to endorse Herbert Farjeon's verdict in the *Daily Herald*: 'As Romeo Mr Olivier was about twenty times as much in love with Juliet as Mr Gielgud is. But Mr Gielgud speaks most of the poetry far better than Mr Olivier. . . . Yet – I must out with it – the fire of Mr Olivier's passion carried the play along as Mr Gielgud's doesn't quite.' Looking back on the production fifteen years later, another critic, J.C. Trewin, clearly felt the same way: 'It was fashionable in those days to hold that Olivier could not speak the verse: he was blamed for his staccato delivery and dry tone. Even so, I thought perversely that his Romeo caressed certain of the lines as no other player in my recollection – not even Gielgud – had done. . . . The actor looked superb: half the battle was won when his Romeo walked upon the New Theatre stage straight from that Verona of hot sun, sharp swords, brief lives, and the nightingale beneath the moon. . . . Olivier was a hearty, swaggering Mercutio; but Romeo is first; it is still his voice that I set to many of the lines in the part, just as Gielgud's voice will always speak my Hamlet and Cassius.'

In rehearsals Gielgud was highly critical of Olivier's delivery, but in performance he was aware that the younger actor was able to achieve a reality in the part that eluded him. 'I bullied him a great deal about his verse-speaking, which, he admitted himself, he wasn't happy about. I was rather showy about mine, and fancied myself very much as a verse speaker, and I became very mannered in consequence. But I was so jealous, because not only did he play Romeo with tremendous energy but he knew just how to cope with it and select. I remember Ralph Richardson saying to me, "But you see, when Larry leans against the balcony and looks up, then you have the whole scene, immediately". . . . I had been draping myself around the stage for weeks, thinking myself very romantic as Romeo, and I was rather baffled and dismayed to find that I couldn't achieve the same effect at all.' Peggy Ashcroft, who, of course, was Juliet to them both, echoed Richardson: 'I thought John's extraordinary, darting imagination made him the better Mercutio, but Larry was the definitive Romeo, a real, vigorous, impulsive youth.'

On one aspect of the production both Gielgud and Olivier were agreed. Neither felt they looked very becoming in tights. Fifty years after the event, Gielgud said to me: 'I hated my legs in those days. Ivor Brown said, "John Gielgud has the most meaningless legs imaginable." He was quite right. Larry hated his legs because they were so thin and I hated mine because they were so knock-kneed.'

Gielgud and Olivier maintained a guarded friendship and professional rivalry for the rest of Olivier's life (more of which anon), but they never appeared together on stage in a play again. Peggy Ashcroft and Edith Evans stayed with Gielgud for his next production for Albery. As *Punch* reported, it was the first full-scale West End production of a Chekhov play. The author 'would surely feel elated could he see with what honour the English stage is handling *The Seagull* now at the New Theatre. A cluster of stars, fully supported, are directed by Komisarjevsky and act in costumes and scenes which omit no detail, that can throw an almost fierce light on the texture of the play. That is the peril of very good acting, that it will show up in the sunlight defects of the dramatist that a less complete mastery of the characters and situations might have left in a kindly blur. But *The Seagull* is full of meat; there are in Chekhov no minor characters: to come on the stage at all is to be a human soul, aspiring and suffering and poignant.' *Punch* was clearly impressed with Komisarjevsky's achievement: 'The mood and the time are brilliantly recaptured and displayed in a masterly production which holds the attention with increasing intensity through four acts and three hours.'

Gielgud, too, admired Komis' overall handling of the play – 'sensational, it really was a most beautiful production' – though at the time he (and several of the critics) had reservations about the way the director had insisted that Gielgud play Trigorin as a dandified gigolo rather than the down-at-heel figure Chekhov himself was known to have envisaged.

The Seagull was a success, but Gielgud was only able to stay in it for six weeks as he was readying himself for his next venture: a new production of *Hamlet*, to be presented on Broadway and directed by Guthrie McClintic, with the film star Lillian Gish as Ophelia, the Australian actress Judith

Anderson (best remembered for her later role as Mrs Danvers in the Hitchcock film of *Rebecca*) as Gertrude and an almost all-American cast. The production opened at the Alexandra Theater, Toronto, in September and came to the St James's Theater in New York in October. The Broadway first night audience was ecstatic; the press was generous, but rather more reserved. The production received an unusual boost from an unexpected quarter when, only a month after it had opened, a rival *Hamlet* starring Leslie Howard also arrived on Broadway. Of the two, John's was undoubtedly the better received and the fortuitous competition between the productions seemed to fuel the public's interest in the play and increase its enthusiasm for the Gielgud interpretation. The New York journal *Stage* awarded its 'Palm' to Gielgud for 'the greatest Prince of Denmark of this generation' and Hamlets of an earlier generation cabled their congratulations. Johnston Forbes-Robertson's wire simply read 'HEARTY CONGRATULATIONS TO MR GIELGUD ON HIS GREAT SUCCESS' but the legendary John Barrymore sent a more extravagant message: 'MY DEAR MR GIELGUD MAY I MOST GLADLY BE ONE OF THE MANY TO CONGRATULATE YOU ON YOUR BRILLIANT SUCCESS . . . ALTHOUGH TO A GREAT EXTENT WE WHO HAVE THE TEMERITY TO ESSAY HIM THINK WE ARE PLAYING HAMLET BUT STRANGELY DIRECT THINKING ON CHARMING PERSON IS IN MANY RESPECTS PLAYING US STOP OCCASIONALLY THIS COMES UNDER THE HEAD OF A TOUGH BREAK AND IT IS NOT ONLY STIMULATING BUT THRILLING THAT YOU HAVE SO SUPERBLY MADE HIM YOUR OWN'.

At the end of the New York run in January 1937, the production went on a brief tour taking in Boston, Philadelphia and Washington DC, where Gielgud and Lillian Gish were invited to the White House, introduced to the

President (who was 'charming, urbane and gracious' according to Gielgud) and given tea by Mrs Roosevelt. By the time he had completed his American run of *Hamlet* Gielgud had given more than 400 performances of the role, but he wasn't finished with it yet.

In 1939 he was invited to give his *Hamlet* in Denmark at the Castle at Elsinore. This time Fay Compton played Ophelia, with Laura Cowie as Gertrude, Jack Hawkins doubling as Claudius and the Ghost, George Howe by now an almost definitive Polonius, Glen Byam Shaw as Horatio, Harry Andrews as Laertes and Marius Goring as the First Player. Before setting off for Denmark, John gave six performances of the play at Sir Henry Irving's old theatre, the Lyceum in Wellington Street. It was the last production staged there before the building was converted into a dance hall. At Elsinore, as in London, the new *Hamlet* was warmly received. The journalist George W. Bishop was there: 'On a calm evening in July, 1939, following a somewhat stormy afternoon, John Gielgud acted Hamlet at Elsinore. I was present when he was greeted on arrival by a salute from two small cannon on the battlements and on the morning following his first performance in the courtyard of Kronborg by the greatest praise in print that probably even he has ever received. The Copenhagen papers were headlined: "The World's Best Hamlet" and the *Berlingske Tidende* described the event as "the biggest occasion in the theatre for years". The dramatic critic of *Politiken* said: "The evening was Gielgud's. Never has English sounded more beautiful from the human mouth."'

The Danish notices for Gielgud were comprehensively glowing. Not so for all the cast. More than half a century after the event, Gielgud liked to tell the story of the fan who followed him to Elsinore. 'She came to every performance and, with her friend, used to move about during the course of the play so that she was always sitting opposite me. One night I changed all my moves to evade her, much to the consternation of my fellow players. The next day my fan came up to our table, when we were having dinner, and said, "I've translated all the reviews for you – I thought you'd like to see them in English." I thanked her and, like a fool, with the entire company sitting round, I started to read the notices out loud. Suddenly, I heard myself saying, "Miss Fay Compton has neither the looks nor the youth of Ophelia, but obviously comes from good theatrical stock." Fay was wonderful and roared with laughter. I felt very shame-faced.'

Gielgud returned to *Hamlet* yet again in 1944, this time with Peggy Ashcroft as Ophelia. Feeling the need for a fresh approach, he didn't direct it himself, but asked the Cambridge don George Rylands, celebrated for his undergraduate productions of Shakespeare, to take on the play. This proved a mistake: the company resented Rylands' didactic approach, and, although many considered this to be John's most successful Hamlet, he wasn't happy with it. He was now forty and conscious of his age. 'I was well aware that, with the help of various directors and actors with whom I'd worked over fifteen years, I knew more about the part, had better staying power, and perhaps more selectivity. But I didn't think I could contrive the opening of the play in the way that it had come to me when I was absolutely fresh, because I really felt it then; I was young and so I naturally put it over in the right way. But later I tried to imitate that, and I felt false.'

He took on the role one last time in 1945, once more in a production of his own, as part of an ENSA tour in the

Middle and Far East.† He played the part for the very last time at the Cairo Opera House in February 1946. Among the young servicemen who saw Gielgud's ENSA *Hamlet* more than once was Donald Sinden. His admiration was unqualified: 'The untold depths of misery he could dredge up in any of Hamlet's lines: the gravity he gave to "A little more than kin, and less than kind". After Hamlet has seen and talked with his father's ghost he says to himself:

> The time is out of joint: O cursed spite,
> That ever I was born to set it right!

'Then he turns to Horatio and Marcellus and says, "Nay, come, let's go together". I wish I could describe how many facets Gielgud gave to that simple line. ("Please go with me." "I don't want to let you out of my sight." "It would look better if we arrived together." "Let us leave this awesome place." "Don't leave me.") I learned from that one line what infinite possibilities are open to an actor.'

Gielgud himself may not have been convinced by the Hamlet he portrayed once he had turned forty, but others had no such reservations. According to Sybil Thorndike, 'Those who saw the Hamlet of John Gielgud have a memory of something hauntingly beautiful for which to be grateful all their lives.' And James Agate had no doubt that the 1944 Hamlet was Gielgud's finest: 'Mr Gielgud is now completely and authoritatively master of this tremendous part. He is, we

---

† Entertainments National Services Association, the official organisation behind the whole range of wartime entertainment for the troops, at home and overseas.

feel, this generation's rightful tenant of this "monstrous Gothic castle of a poem". He has acquired an almost Irvingesque quality of pathos, and in the passages after the play scene an incisiveness, a raillery, a mordancy worthy of the Old Man. He imposes on us this play's questing feverishness. The middle act gives us ninety minutes of high excitement and assured virtuosity; Forbes-Robertson was not more bedazzling in the "O, what a rogue and peasant slave" soliloquy. In short, I hold that this is, and is likely to remain, the best Hamlet of our time.'

five

'THE FINEST FLOWER OF THE CONTEMPORARY STAGE'
1934–1948

For a complete man of the theatre – as Gielgud certainly was by the mid-1930s – his first forays into management were surprisingly unlucky. In 1933, Emlyn Williams, then twenty-eight and as much a playwright as an actor, had sent him his latest work, *Spring 1600*. John liked the play and wanted to direct it. When Bronson Albery said it was one that he didn't want to produce, Gielgud decided to turn impresario and, together with his good friend Richard Clowes (whose father nobly offered to help secure the financial backing), presented the play at the Shaftesbury in January 1934. It was an elaborate production, costing £4,000 plus – with ambitious settings designed by Motley, a large number of walk-ons in addition to the not uncostly cast (including a monkey), a chorus of singers and a substantial orchestra – and in the event proved to be an expensive flop. The dress rehearsal prompted one of Gielgud's famous gaffes. Armed with a megaphone, the director addressed the company from the front of the dress circle: 'The last act is terribly thin. We must try to make the best of it.' From the darkened stalls, Emlyn Williams' voice responded, 'We all know the last act is thin, John, but you needn't announce the fact to the entire cast. You might wait for the critics to do that.' As it turned out, despite the insubstantial last act and the length of the evening (three and a half hours), the notices were fair-to-middling, but, even so, the customers didn't come and the show closed after a few weeks.

A year later Rodney Ackland brought Gielgud his adaptation of Hugh Walpole's novel, *The Old Ladies*. Again, Gielgud liked it, wanted to direct it, and when Albery declined to become involved, teamed up once more with Richard Clowes (and his munificent father) and presented it himself, first at the New Theatre, then at the smaller St Martin's. The production was less expensive and the notices creditable ('Not for months have I heard any audience cheer as last night's did' – W.A. Darlington). But business was poor and again the play only survived a matter of weeks.

In the spring of 1937, immediately after the American tour of *Hamlet*, Gielgud produced a second play by Emlyn Williams, this time in partnership with the author. Williams had written *He Was Born Gay* specially for Gielgud. Since the subject was the life in England of Louis XV's lost son, 'a romantic half-mad princeling', and Gielgud was ready to star in the piece as well as co-present and co-direct it, from the commercial viewpoint the project looked more promising than either of its predecessors. In fact, it was the least successful of the three. After a short pre-London tour the play opened at the Queen's on 26 May 1937, only to close within a fortnight, after just twelve performances, giving Gielgud the shortest run of his career.

Having failed conspicuously with three new plays, for his next managerial enterprise Gielgud turned back to the classics, to dead authors whose worth and work and popularity with the public he could more readily rely on. In the early summer of 1937 he decided the time was right to attempt to realise an ambition he had been nurturing for several years: to form his own permanent company and present a full season of plays in London under his own management. At the end of the season, Michel Saint-Denis who was involved in the venture, described its genesis: 'The idea of forming a permanent company did not occur to Gielgud suddenly. He was already talking about it when I produced *Noah* with him. It took shape slowly during the four years of his work at the New Theatre and culminated with the success of *The Seagull*, produced by Komisarjevsky. The nucleus of the company was, in fact, formed at that time. He surrounded himself with first-class actors and a group of very capable and enthusiastic young actors. He did not try to show himself as a solo actor. He cared more about the ensemble. He invited Tyrone Guthrie and Komisarjevsky to produce for him. Then, because Komisarjevsky was not free, I was asked. He chose four strong classical plays of different styles for his repertory. The public would be able to watch the same actors in their interpretation of great characters of various periods. The plays were put on for eight weeks minimum and ten weeks maximum. Each producer was offered the possibility of seven or nine weeks rehearsals. Security was given to the actors for a period of nine months. The leading members of the cast worked on a percentage basis, and so did the guest-actors who were specially engaged for one or more plays during the course of the season. Thus it was made possible for a large number of leading actors to work together.'

Living as we do in the age of subsidised national companies where an eight-week rehearsal period for a play is considered commonplace, it is difficult to appreciate how revolutionary Gielgud's enterprise was. At the Old Vic the company might remain the same for a season, but the plays were rehearsed in three weeks. In the commercial theatre, a cast was brought together for each individual play, rehearsed for three weeks and perhaps given a brief pre-London tour before embarking on an as-long-as-possible West End run. There were other actor-managers who produced a repertoire of plays with the same company, but usually with the notion of presenting themselves as the star attraction and not with the ideal of creating an 'ensemble'. In retrospect it is easy to take Gielgud's 1937/38 season at the Queen's almost for granted, to dismiss it as simply a successful quartet of plays with all-star casts and so fail to recognise it for the pioneering achievement it was. At the time – several years before the Olivier/Richardson Old Vic seasons at the New Theatre after the war and many years before the creation of the Royal Shakespeare Company and the National Theatre – Saint-Denis was one of those who realised that the achievements of 1937/38 would have 'important consequences'. He put it very simply: 'If good work was done it was because the conditions of work were so much better than in the average theatre.'

And good work certainly was done. The season opened and closed with Shakespeare, *Richard II* and *The Merchant of Venice*, with *The School for Scandal* and *The Three Sisters* in between. The plays were scheduled to run for eight to ten weeks preceded by up to nine weeks of rehearsals. Most of the actors had never known such luxury, indeed regarded it as a self-indulgence, but all were convinced by the experience. Gwen Ffrangcon-Davies, who, with Angela Baddeley and Carol Goodner, was one of the guest stars engaged to appear in only one or two of the plays, was apprehensive before rehearsals began, but after seven weeks admitted, 'I have never had the opportunity of working for such a long time. I thought I would be stale, but on the contrary, it changes one's whole attitude to one's work.'

The company was a fine one, led by Gielgud himself, who appeared in all four plays, with Peggy Ashcroft, other old friends like George Howe, Leon Quartermaine and Harcourt Williams, plus younger players like George Devine, Harry Andrews, Anthony Quayle, Alec Guinness and Michael Redgrave. Gielgud launched the season with *Richard II*, directing as well as playing the title role, because it was a part he knew well and could approach with confidence. 'John, even at the first reading, was as near perfect as I could wish or imagine,' Michael Redgrave, who played Bolingbroke, recalled. 'Ninety per cent of the beauty of his acting was the beauty of his voice. To this day I can see no way of improving on the dazzling virtuosity of phrasing and breathing which was Gielgud's in the cadenza beginning:

> Draw near,
> And list what with our council we have done. . . .'

Some critics found fault with Motley's over-decorated settings (and a few of Gielgud's friends found fault with his over-decorated performance: 'Act on the lines, not in between them,' said Harley Granville-Barker), but overall the production was acclaimed. The eulogy in the *Illustrated Sporting and Dramatic News* was not untypical: 'The season which John Gielgud has begun so auspiciously by presenting, producing and playing *Richard II*, bids fair to be the most important that the English Theatre has known for some years. Unlike the actor-managers of tradition, Mr Gielgud chooses to surround himself with the finest flower of the contemporary stage; and advisedly, for he can pit his genius against the greatest odds. The greatest odds, on this occasion, took the form of Leon Quartermaine who, as John of Gaunt, gave a towering performance which already had become a legend by the time the curtain fell.'

The School for Scandal was given a cooler reception. Gielgud presented a deliberately unsympathetic Joseph Surface, which some of his loyal followers found uncomfortable. The production, too, directed by Tyrone Guthrie and designed, apparently, 'to show the itch beneath the powder', came in for criticism: some saw it as too busy and contrived, others as too earthy and mundane.

Michel Saint-Denis's version of *The Three Sisters*, on the other hand, was universally hailed as a masterpiece. Herbert Farjeon spoke for all: 'It is in the order of things that a critic should praise this play. It is in the order of things that an audience, to signify appreciation, should applaud the perfectest herald of joy. One is so overwhelmed by the poignant beauty of the production that anything written or spoken must fall far short of what one feels. Moreover, the emotional reaction is so personal, so private, that one is in no mood for eloquence . . . If Mr Gielgud's season at the Queen's had produced only this, it would have more than justified itself. There is a tenderness in the acting so exquisite that it is like the passing of light . . . Here, in short, is a production of the very first order of one of the masterpieces of dramatic literature.'

Gielgud admired the production ('Remarkable. Really stunning. Everybody said it was the best Chekhovian production that has ever been done in this country') though he didn't consider his own performance as Colonel Vershinin totally satisfactory. Nor, in the production that closed the season, was Gielgud very happy with his own Shylock, played not in the heroic Irving tradition, but as a shuffling, morose, malignant outsider. The public might have preferred something on a grander, less vulnerable, less credible scale, but many of Gielgud's colleagues – Olivier among them – regarded it as one of his finest characterisations.

By the time he came to play Shylock, and co-direct the play with Glen Byam Shaw, Gielgud was weary. Though satisfying and gratifying – and even profitable† – it had been a long, heavy season and when it came to an end and the company disbanded, John was happy to slough off his

---

† According to Gielgud, 'This season in management was a financial success, although the four productions had each of them to be paid for in advance before I knew whether the current play would show a profit. The most expensive production cost £2,200 (*The Three Sisters*), the least expensive £1,700, and of the four plays presented only the Chekhov was a very great success.'

managerial yoke for a while and accept a handsome offer to
star with Dame Marie Tempest in Dodie Smith's family
comedy, *Dear Octopus*, again directed by Byam Shaw. The
invitation came from Hugh 'Binkie' Beaumont, whom
Gielgud had first met more than a decade before when Binkie
had been the business manager at Barnes and Gielgud had
appeared in the Russian season there. Beaumont was now
twenty-nine, the newly appointed managing director of
H.M. Tennent, destined to be London's most influential and
respected commercial management for a quarter of a
century, during which time he remained one of Gielgud's
closest friends and professional advisers, as well as being his
most frequent employer.

Binkie Beaumont had put £1,000 into the Gielgud season
at the Queen's Theatre. The principal backers, investing
£5,000 apiece, were Gielgud himself and his friend and flat-
mate, John Perry. Perry (whose money came from his
prosperous Irish family) was a handsome young actor in the
Gielgud mould (in terms of manner at least, if not in skill or
achievement). When Gielgud left his parents' home in the
early 1920s, he moved first into a flat in Mecklenburgh
Square, WC1, near Russell Square (borrowed from another
actor friend, George Howe), and then took a lease of his own
on a more convenient fourth-floor flat at Seven Dials, off
St Martin's Lane, near Cambridge Circus. Gielgud invited
Perry to share the flat with him and they lived together there
and, later, in St John's Wood. Then, when Gielgud's growing
success made it possible, they shared his country house at
Henley, until Perry met and fell for Binkie Beaumont, when
he moved out of the Gielgud residences and into the
Beaumont ones. The three men remained close all their lives.

Before embarking on the rehearsals for *Dear Octopus*, Gielgud had directed *Spring Meeting*, a play with an Irish setting, starring Margaret Rutherford and written by John Perry with Molly Skrine (better known then as M.J. Farrell and now as Molly Keane). Over the next decade Gielgud directed another eight plays (usually for the H.M. Tennent management) in which he didn't appear himself; the most notable was probably *The Beggar's Opera* at the Haymarket in the spring of 1940, with Michael Redgrave leading a Glyndebourne company. When Redgrave was ill, Gielgud went on and sang Macheath himself for four performances. Nobody asked for their money back.

Dear Octopus was a considerable commercial success for Beaumont and H.M. Tennent. The piece may have been a slight, sentimental comedy – and Gielgud may not have cared for his character ('rather a dull, conventional, juvenile') – but the public seemed happy enough and Gielgud stayed in the play for eleven months from August 1938 to June 1939. Many years later, I asked him what he remembered about it. 'Principally the first night,' he said. 'It coincided with Munich. I remember at the party afterwards Noel Coward arrived, ashen-faced, saying this was the most terrible thing that had happened. We didn't know what he was talking about. We were all waving our champagne glasses and toasting Mr Chamberlain's piece of paper and his promise of "peace in our time".'

What was his co-star Marie Tempest like? 'Short, plump, no great beauty, but she had style. She played herself in every part, coming on in a series of chic outfits, with beautiful shoes and crisp little hats, always wonderfully *soignée*. Though she didn't get along with Dodie Smith very well, she was just right for *Dear Octopus*. It was a charming, cosy little play and people loved it. They didn't want to think about the possibility of war.'

Nor did Gielgud. The clouds might be gathering menacingly over Europe, but for John G, as he was always known to his friends, the affairs of nations always came a poor second to the world of the theatre which was and would always be his universe. It was during these uneasy days before the outbreak of war that he went to stay with the writer Beverley Nichols. 'He arrived on an evening of acute international tension,' according to Nichols. 'We were sitting round in a state of unaccustomed gloom, wondering what was going to happen to us all, whether we should be able to finish our books or our poems or our paintings or our music, or whether we were all going to be swept up in the approaching holocaust. "If you're all so worried about what's going to happen," said John, "why don't you turn on the radio?" "There isn't one," I said. "That," replied John, "is excellent news, because I shall be able to listen to myself talking . . ." And talk he did, brilliantly, till the small hours of the morning – not about Hitler or Mussolini or any of the other ogres who were haunting us, but about the theatre, which was all he knew about or thought important in this distracted world.

'On the following morning I rose early, to get the papers from the village post office. But I found that John had forestalled me. He was sitting in the music room, surrounded by scattered copies of the Sunday papers, whose headlines were double-decked with disaster. Ultimatums, troop movements, diplomatic scurryings, mobilisations. His face was dark.

'"What in heaven's name has happened?", I demanded.

'His face grew darker. But he had not noticed the head-lines. He was scanning the theatrical pages.

'"The worst," he proclaimed in sepulchral tones. "Gladys has got the most appalling notices. And so has the play." He strode to the window and stared out. "I don't know what the world is coming to."'†

When the war came, Gielgud was anxious to be of service, but did not see himself quite in the front line. Kitty Black, working for Binkie Beaumont at H.M. Tennent, recalled the reaction to the possibility of John G going off to war: 'Suddenly one morning there was a tremendous flurry in the office. John Gielgud had been passed A1 at his medical examination and his call-up papers had come through. The idea of losing England's leading actor was absolutely unthinkable, quite apart from the fact that he would probably prove useless at anything practical in the military line. Binkie had assured him he would never have to get into uniform and now sprang into action. He discovered the right office to approach and scuttled off to Hobart House in Grosvenor Gardens, emerging triumphantly with an order granting John exemption for the duration (I can never drive that way to Victoria without a *frisson* as I remember that narrow squeak), and as a result John declared that he would only appear in the classics for the rest of the war.'

---

† This is how Beverley Nichols told me the story and how he recounts it in *The Unforgiving Minute*, one of his volumes of autobiography. However, Ronald Cook is one of several people who tell me that, at the time, Gielgud's line was reported to be 'Jimmy Agate has given Edith [Evans] the most *terrible* notice.'

This self-denying ordinance meant abandoning plans to play Maxim de Winter in the stage version of *Rebecca* (he was rehearsing the part on the day war was declared) and turning his attention to revivals of *Hamlet* (at the Lyceum in London and at Elsinore Castle in Denmark) and *The Importance of Being Earnest* at the Globe.[†]

Because it was with *Hamlet* that Henry Irving (with Ellen Terry as Ophelia) had inaugurated his celebrated reign at the Lyceum in 1878, it was felt fitting that *Hamlet* with John Gielgud (and Fay Compton as Ophelia) should bring the historic theatre's life as a playhouse to a close in June 1939.[‡] After six special farewell performances at the Lyceum, Gielgud took his production off to Denmark in July to present Shakespeare's tragedy in the courtyard of the castle which is its historical setting. The Elsinore *Hamlet* Festival had been inaugurated the year before with a visit from the Old Vic Company, with Laurence Olivier as Hamlet (and Vivien Leigh as Ophelia) in Tyrone Guthrie's production. (Famously, Gielgud went backstage after the opening night of Olivier's first *Hamlet* in 1937 and said, 'Larry, it's one of the finest performances I have ever seen, but it's still my part.')

In *The Importance of Being Earnest* Gielgud again played John Worthing, with Ronald Ward as Algernon, Joyce Carey and Angela Baddeley as Gwendolyn and Cecily, and Edith Evans giving what is generally accepted as the definitive Lady

---

[†] This marked the beginning of Gielgud's long association with the theatre in Shaftesbury Avenue. On 2 November 1994, with Sir John in attendance, the Globe was renamed the Gielgud in his honour.

[‡] The Lyceum enjoyed five decades as a dance hall before becoming a playhouse again in the 1990s.

Bracknell. Gielgud revived the production in 1941, again at the Globe and again with Edith Evans, but with Jack Hawkins as Algernon and Gwen Ffrangcon-Davies and Peggy Ashcroft as the girls. Of the 1939 production *The Times* declared, 'If the past theatrical decade had to be represented by a single production, this is the one that many good judges would choose.' And Tyrone Guthrie, not a man readily given to hyperbole, spoke of the 1941 revival 'establishing the high water mark of artificial comedy in our era'.

A year later, at the Phoenix, Gielgud revived the play once more, with the same trio of leading ladies, but with Cyril Ritchard in place of Jack Hawkins and Jean Cadell now replacing Margaret Rutherford as Miss Prism. His final revival was a production he took to Canada and the United States in 1947, this time with Margaret Rutherford as a much less imperious Lady Bracknell, Robert Flemyng as Algy and Pamela Brown and Jane Baxter as the girls. When it opened at the Royale in New York, the play was as warmly welcomed as the earlier English revivals had been, though Gielgud realised by now that it was a piece which didn't benefit from long runs: 'When we played it too long and lost the inner feeling of fun, it wasn't funny any more. This was interesting, because it has to be played with the most enormous solemnity. But inside you play the whole play as if you were doing a practical joke – with immense seriousness, knowing yourself that you are being killingly funny. And yet if you were to betray with the slightest flicker of an eyelash that you know you're funny, you are not funny either. When we lost the inner fun after six or eight months – when we got sick of the play – it immediately told and the play became a sort of affected exercise.'

In the spring of 1940, with the first revival of *The Importance* and the Redgrave *Beggar's Opera* behind him, Gielgud returned to the Old Vic for the first time in almost a decade. With Tyrone Guthrie and Lewis Casson as his collaborators, he presented a short season of Shakespeare – *King Lear* and *The Tempest* – with a distinguished company including Jessica Tandy, Fay Compton, Cathleen Nesbitt, Robert Harris, Jack Hawkins and Marius Goring. Harley Granville-Barker, now sixty-three, playwright, author, director and much-revered man of the theatre (in 1910 John Masefield had told him, 'People have come to regard you as a kind of god'), was invited over from his home in Paris to direct *Lear*. He declined to take full command or to have his name on the billing, but agreed to come and work with the company for about ten days. For Gielgud, 'they were the fullest in experience that I have ever had in all my years upon the stage.' Looking back on that time twenty-five years later Gielgud described Granville-Barker's working methods: 'He used to come every day to the Vic and rehearse, looking like a marvellous surgeon. The company was transported. I never saw actors watch a director with such utter admiration and obedience. It was like Toscanini coming to rehearsal – very quiet, business suit, eyebrows, and text in his hand. And I was so angry because there was nobody there to take his overcoat, or take notes for him, and he filled every moment; so much so that people didn't even go to try on their wigs, or have a bun, or anything – they sat there. I got actors and actresses, from outside, friends of mine, to come and peek in, because I said "You really must see these rehearsals, they're something absolutely extraordinary." And we would go on until quite late at night. I remember doing the death scene of

Lear with him, and he began by stopping me on every word, and I thought every moment he'd say, "Now stop, don't act any more, we'll just work it out for technical effects." Not at all, he didn't say stop, so I went on acting and crying and carrying on, and trying to take the corrections as he gave them to me. And when I looked at my watch, we had been working on this short scene for forty minutes. But it was extraordinary that he had the skill not to make you wild and not to exhaust you so much that you couldn't go on; if you had the strength to go along with him, he could give you more than any person I ever met in my life.'

When they began work on the play together Granville-Barker had told Gielgud, 'Lear should be an oak, you're an ash; now we've got to do something about that.' The play was generally well received, though not all the critics felt that Gielgud's Lear was sufficiently the oak. Granville-Barker himself was well satisfied with his pupil's achievement. On 14 April 1940, Gielgud's thirty-sixth birthday, he wrote to him:

> The Athenaeum,
> Pall Mall, SW1
> Sunday morning

My dear Gielgud, Lear is in your grasp.

Forget all the things I have bothered you about. Let your own now well-disciplined instincts carry you along, and up: simply allowing the checks and changes to prevent your being carried *away*. And I prophesy – happily – great things for you.

> Yrs,
> HGB

The Times described the production as 'the first genuine theatrical occasion of the war'. The fall of France coincided with the Old Vic season and Gielgud was conscious of the fact that what he called 'the smell of the times' both infected the play and enhanced the audience's receptivity to it: 'People used to come around and say, "This play is absolutely extraordinary, it's given us such pride," and I'd say, "But how can you bear it – this tearing out of the eyes, the death of the king, the cruelty . . ." But they would say, "Well, there's a kind of catharsis, and when we come out of the theatre we are uplifted, like after hearing Beethoven. It shows that with all the appalling horror that is going on – there is some glory, and something that's worth everything." This seemed to me extraordinary, and I felt it so deeply; we all did in the company at that time.'

Lear was followed by *The Tempest* with Gielgud's Prospero, 'a scholarly Italian nobleman', in a production directed by George Devine and Marius Goring (and without assistance from Granville-Barker) that was well regarded. *The Tempest* was to be the Old Vic's last play for a decade. Shortly after the end of the run on 22 June 1940, the theatre was bombed and did not reopen until 1950.

Gielgud's next contribution to the war effort took the form of a series of lectures devised by Ivor Brown entitled 'Shakespeare – in Peace and War' (a talk-cum-recital that culminated with the show-stopping 'Once more unto the breach' speech from *Henry V*) followed by a tour of military bases with a programme of three short pieces: *Fumed Oak* and *Hands Across the Sea*, two of the one-act plays from Noel Coward's *Tonight at 8.30* sequence, and *Hard Luck Story*, Gielgud's own adaptation of Chekhov's playlet *Swan Song* about an old actor rehearsing in a deserted theatre with only an ancient prompter for an audience.

In the winter of 1940 he made another film, *The Prime Minister*, an indifferent historical pageant about the life and times of Benjamin Disraeli, in which Gielgud neither imitated nor rivalled George Arliss's definitive screen portrayal of the same character. Immediately the film was completed (it was shot in forty-eight days at Teddington), Gielgud returned to the war-ravaged West End where many of the theatres that had chosen not to close at the onset of war and then been forced to close during the worst of the Blitz, were now doing their best to maintain a policy of 'business as usual'. The vehicle Gielgud chose for himself was J.M. Barrie's gentle fantasy *Dear Brutus*, which had enjoyed its first success during the Great War. As theatre it may be fairly flimsy, 'no more than a whimsey', but the public took to it and it ran at the Globe from January to May, when John took it on tour, first commercially, then for ENSA.†

Also for ENSA, in the winter of 1942, Gielgud joined Beatrice Lillie and Edith Evans in a revue called *Christmas Party* which they took to Gibraltar to entertain the troops stationed there. They gave forty-eight performances in the small garrison theatre and concerts on board an assortment of battleships and aircraft carriers. Gielgud kept the Commander's announcement of their visit to HMS *Nelson*:

---

† *Dear Brutus* was not obvious fare for the average serviceman. According to Kitty Black, when the production reached a Canadian forces' camp at Borden, the play's 'dream child' sequence provoked 'a loud scraping of boots' as half the audience left, one of them muttering, 'Jesus Christ, they're crackers.'

PERSONAL VISIT

OF

JOHN GIELGUD & CO TO HMS NELSON

BEATRICE LILLIE   EDITH EVANS

ELISABETH WELCH   JEANNE DE CASALIS

PHYLLIS STANLEY   MICHAEL WILDING

JOHN GIELGUD

A short show starting at 1400. Rig – Dress of the Day, or working rig for men on duty or who cannot shift. The Dress of the Day is being made No 3's after dinner as a compliment to the artistes. PLEASE REMEMBER TO KEEP THE STAGE, SEATING AND DECKS CLEAN DURING THE DINNER HOUR AS THERE WILL BE NOBODY TO SWEEP UP BEFORE THE SHOW. Loudspeakers are being rigged so that any audience in the octopidal should be able to hear.

MR GIELGUD HAS PROMISED TO GIVE US HIS RENDERING OF "NELSON'S SPIRIT" – LET US SHOW HIM AND HIS COMPANY OURS.

In 1942 and 1943 Gielgud also returned to two of the roles he had first played in his twenties: Macbeth, and Valentine in Congreve's *Love for Love*. He found this second Macbeth less satisfactory than his first in 1930. It was persuasive but not towering, again the timber was wrong. The actor and writer Robert Speaight was not alone in applauding the 'imaginative intensity' and 'deep psychological insight', while feeling 'only the warrior's muscle was missing'. After seeing the performance, James Agate wrote in his journal: 'John will never be happy vocally with Macbeth; his voice is neither deep enough nor resonant enough. But what sheer acting ability can do, he does. He is the only Macbeth I have ever seen who has kept it up all the way through; the last act, where most of them fall down, is superb.'

Gielgud told me he was not happy with *Macbeth* this time around: 'It was exhausting and not very successful. In 1942 I played it for nearly a whole year, a long, long time, considering it is such a desperately difficult play and traditionally so very unlucky.' At the lunch marking Sir John's eightieth birthday, the actress Constance Cummings took issue with Gielgud's own verdict on his performance: 'John transcended whatever difficulties have plagued other actors in the part. He took it at such a pace. He played it as a man of action and the character's misgivings were never allowed to turn him from his purpose. There was a wonderful tension in his performance, right the way through.'

If opinions of his Macbeth varied, praise for his second attempt at Valentine in *Love for Love* was universal. Among its numerous avid admirers was the precocious Kenneth Tynan who saw it, aged seventeen, and reported: 'Tongue-in-cheek and hand-on-heart, he played the mock-madness scenes as a sort of burlesque of his own Hamlet: he extended the intense raptness, the silent inner lightnings which he shares with Irving, until they reached delicious absurdity. Gielgud is an actor who refuses to compromise with his audience: he does not offer a welcoming hand, but binds a spell instead.'

Gielgud played Valentine on tour in the spring of 1943 and then for a year's run in the West End, at the Phoenix and the Haymarket. With *Hamlet* once more and Somerset Maugham's *The Circle* (in which he loved playing and was much acclaimed as 'the furniture-conscious prim husband' Arnold Champion-Cheyney), he revived *Love for Love* in the summer of 1944 for a further tour and a season at the Haymarket. The same season – billed as 'John Gielgud's Repertory' – continued in early 1945 with *A Midsummer Night's Dream*: Gielgud and Peggy Ashcroft were Oberon and Titania in what was recognised as a heavy-handed production by the Oxford don Nevill Coghill. This was followed by *The Duchess of Malfi*, Webster's oppressive and, to Gielgud certainly, unsympathetic Jacobean tragedy, directed with little verve by George Rylands, Cambridge's answer to Nevill Coghill.

Gielgud's war culminated in the autumn of 1945 with a long tour of the Middle and Far East, playing *Hamlet* for the fifth and final time and Charles Condomine in Coward's *Blithe Spirit* for the first and last. At the end of the wearying tour – eighty shows in eighteen weeks plus his recital of 'Shakespeare – In Peace and War' – Gielgud returned with plans to direct Robert Helpmann in Rodney Ackland's dramatisation of Dostoevsky's *Crime and Punishment*. In the event, Helpmann was taken ill, so Gielgud agreed to play Raskolnikoff and Anthony Quayle took over as director. Edith Evans played Madame Marmaladoff and Peter Ustinov the Chief of Police.

In his autobiography Ustinov paints a revealing picture of Gielgud at the time, touching on the curious mixture of shyness and vanity that were hallmarks of the man: 'John Gielgud is so contorted with shyness at first meetings that he makes a normally shy person like myself feel brash, and even boorish. And yet, despite this gossamer delicacy, there are the heights to rise to before an anonymous public, and an ego, totally invisible in the drawing-room, imperceptibly takes over. As the curtain fell on the first act of *Crime and Punishment* during the first performance, he suddenly trumpeted a message to us all: "If there are going to have to be all these people in the wings, they must look at me!" He found it impossible to play to backs turned in discretion, in order not to break his concentration. To hell with the concentration, once there were people he was hungry for faces!'

Crime and Punishment was tolerably received by most critics and enthusiastically by some. Agate declared that Gielgud's Raskolnikoff was 'the best thing after Hamlet he has ever given us.'

At the beginning of 1947 Gielgud set off for Canada and the United States. He spent the next eighteen months there, playing in *The Importance, Love for Love, Crime and Punishment* (unsatisfactorily redirected by Komisarjevsky who rather despised the piece) and directing Judith Anderson and playing opposite her in a new version of Euripides' *Medea*, in which she scored a personal success but he didn't. When he returned to England in the middle of 1948 – scotching rumours that he had abandoned the British theatre for good and was seeking American citizenship – he directed three plays in as many months, none of which enjoyed any great success, and then chose to make his West End comeback in St John Hankin's appropriately entitled but unhappily dated *The Return of the Prodigal*. It was not much of a success either.

Gielgud's fortunes were at a low ebb. He was still a great star, of course, never short of offers and lucrative ones at that, but he was aware that he had lost his sense of direction

and, whereas a few years before, he had been the un-
challenged leader of the profession, the reins had now
slipped from his fingers. When Laurence Olivier played
Richard III in the first of several glorious Old Vic seasons at
the New Theatre in 1944, with characteristically impetuous
generosity Gielgud had sent him the sword that the great
Edmund Kean had used as Richard, the same sword that had
been presented to Henry Irving on his first night in the role,
the sword that John Gielgud's mother had passed on to him
in his turn. Giving the sword to Olivier had in no sense been
intended as a symbolic gesture, but Gielgud could not fail to
recognise Olivier's ascendant star.

When Gielgud returned to England, Olivier, who was three
years his junior, had recently been knighted, had just
completed his film of *Hamlet*, and was enjoying the kind of
sustained critical acclaim Gielgud had not known in ten
years. For Gielgud, the most generous and giving of men, it
was a perplexing and uncertain time. Peggy Ashcroft used to
tell an endearing story about him. Gielgud was discussing
Othello. 'I don't really know what jealousy is,' he said. Then
he caught himself. 'Oh, yes, I do! I remember! When Larry
had a success as Hamlet I wept.'

six

HONOUR – AND HUMILIATION
1949–1958

'Gielgud has new chance of No 1 place' ran a headline in the London *Evening Standard* in the spring of 1949. The article was prompted by the news that John was to star in Christopher Fry's latest play *The Lady's Not for Burning* and declared in no uncertain terms, 'Olivier is a first class actor and producer. But in my opinion Gielgud is the one genius of the contemporary English stage.'

Whether or not Gielgud's genius was put fully to the test in Fry's medieval verse comedy is debatable, but that Thomas Mendip provided him with his strongest role in a new play since *Richard of Bordeaux*, and his first considerable success in several years, was beyond dispute. The play was written for Alec Clunes who played it originally at the Arts Theatre. Kitty Black, from the H.M. Tennent office, was one of those who went to see it there. Immediately, she wrote to Gielgud: 'I cried all the time because it wasn't your voice speaking the lines.' Beaumont and Gielgud agreed it might make a marvellous vehicle for John and Alec Clunes nobly relinquished the part on the grounds, according to Kitty Black, 'that it was in the author's best interests to do so'. Clunes maintained that in giving up the play, he had 'performed the most self-sacrificing action of his artistic career'. That he was persuaded to do so is a reminder of the effortless authority of John Gielgud as a star and the awesome power of Binkie Beaumont as a manager at the time.

In rehearsal and on tour, Gielgud had growing reservations about the play's chances of success and, with Fry, continued to work on the structure of the piece right up to the London first night – and beyond. Gielgud's fears, however, proved unfounded. The play – with an evocative setting by Oliver Messel and a strong cast, including Pamela Brown, Esme Percy, Harcourt Williams, an eighteen-year-old Claire Bloom and a twenty-four-year-old Richard Burton – was an immediate success with critics and public alike, both in London in 1949 and again in New York two years later. Kenneth Tynan, now all of twenty-two, was one of those who enthused gently over the production, especially over Gielgud's handling of the verse: 'Gielgud, incomparably alert to Fry's poetry, demonstrated in *The Lady's Not For Burning* that here at least was dramatic verse which could be spoken at the speed of dramatic prose: not cryptic and solemn, needing sombre pointing and emphases, but trickling, skimming, darting like a salmon in a mountain stream. Mr Gielgud's company spoke better than any other group of players in England; and for this the credit must be his.'

1949 represented a turning-point in Gielgud's fortunes in another, perhaps even more significant, way. Anthony Quayle had recently been appointed director of the

Shakespeare Memorial Theatre at Stratford-upon-Avon and he now invited Gielgud to come to work at Stratford for the first time, to direct Diana Wynyard and Quayle himself as Beatrice and Benedick in *Much Ado About Nothing*. Gielgud leapt at the opportunity and with a fine company (the walk-ons, 'Watchmen, servants and dancers', included Jill Bennett, Margaret Courtenay, Michael Bates, Robert Hardy and Robert Shaw) gave the play a clear, dynamic and witty production that heralded his return to work of real substance, tackled with a lightness of touch and sureness of hand.

For the 1950 Stratford season, Gielgud revived and refined the production and played in it himself, with Peggy Ashcroft as his Beatrice. It was nothing short of a triumph. J.C. Trewin was there: 'Applause in a theatre, when it is earned, is to me as the spirit-stirring drum was to Othello. It is, I know, unfashionable in these days to show excitement. Rather, we should be ready to tilt the acid, light the fuse. Attack must come before appreciation. The theatre is a kind of blood-sport, with the actors as Early Christians and ourselves as ravenous lions. Absurd! Nothing enlivens the theatre more than enthusiasm, not hysterical, good-old-Tommy "fan" cheers, or a salute to any average lounge-set, but the crash of applause from an audience that is delighted, and sometimes stirred profoundly.

'That kind of cheering followed the fall of the Stratford-upon-Avon curtain on John Gielgud's revival of *Much Ado About Nothing* . . . John Gielgud's Benedick woos us in festival terms. His return to full stature as a Shakespearean has lodged the season safely in the records . . . It was an evening of clear excitement. Now that Benedick is back in Gielgud's repertory, he should remain there.'

And remain there he did for several years. Gielgud played him again in London in 1952 with Diana Wynyard as Beatrice, in London and on the continent in 1955 with Peggy Ashcroft, and finally in the United States in 1959 with Margaret Leighton. He spoke of all three Beatrices with affection: Leighton was 'absolutely enchanting'; Wynyard played it 'along the lines I imagine Ellen Terry did – the great lady, sweeping about in beautiful clothes'; Ashcroft was 'most original – almost with a touch of Beatrice Lillie'. Ashcroft gave her own description of playing with Gielgud in *Much Ado*: 'It was like following your partner so that you never quite knew which steps you were going to take but you could always respond since you were so in tune.'

In *The Many Faces of Gielgud*, the actor Clive Francis collected two particularly telling vignettes from players who appeared in *Much Ado* when it came to London. First, Robert Hardy:

> London 1952: 'Why don't you come and play Claudio for me?' I joined his company for the record-breaking run of *Much Ado* at the Phoenix. Gielgud's Benedick, Wynyard's Beatrice, Scofield's Don Pedro, Tutin's Hero, Lewis Casson, George Rose, Brewster Mason . . . After a night out, I overslept, and woke thirty-five minutes before a matinee two miles away; got a taxi, arrived at the Phoenix ten minutes before curtain up, sweating, quaking, dry-mouthed. Gielgud said, almost with a grin, 'There you are . . . rather naughty . . . take your time.' They held the curtain. Half ready in the wings, like a walking corpse, I heard his voice behind me: 'Try not to worry . . . do relax . . . and remember to think of me as Benedick, not

John Gielgud . . . It will never do, you know, if you are all tense and hunched . . . just think of yourself as a Renaissance princeling . . . take a leaf out of my book.'

Next, Dorothy Tutin:

I was thrilled to be offered Hero when John's famous production of *Much Ado About Nothing* came from Stratford to London. I had been told he always had many ideas so it was best to be 'open' to anything. He was quite brilliant as Benedick, the wittiest I have ever seen, but the Hero scene tricking Beatrice that Benedick was in love with her obviously bored him as much as it terrified me. Finally, he exploded in exasperation and said, 'Oh dear, this is all dreadfully *dull* – give the poor girl a fan – or something.' I was presented with a period thing and waved it about and he said, 'Oh good. That's much better.' And never another note I had.

Thanks to Gielgud's presence at the head of the company and to his potency at the box office, the 1950 season at Stratford began a month earlier than in previous years. Gielgud himself regarded it as a turning-point: 'I had what amounted to a fresh start in a glorious season at Stratford, playing four parts – Angelo, Cassius, Benedick and King Lear.' The opening production was the twenty-five year old Peter Brook's *Measure for Measure* in which Gielgud gave a haunting, steel-hard portrayal of Angelo, 'discovering new depths of feeling and ranges of voice' (T.C. Worsley) in an unromantic role that a few years before he might have felt was too unsympathetic for him to want to tackle.

Brook later described Gielgud as 'a mass of contradictions': 'There is in him an actor-reactor, quick on the draw, answering before the question is put, highly strung, confusing and ever so impatient. Yet tempering his John-in-perpetual-motion is the John-of-intuitions, who winces at every success, his own or others.' Thirty years after the event, Brook looked back on their first collaboration: 'I found that the most important time was just before the first performance, when I had to help him ruthlessly to scrap ninety per cent of his over-rich material and remind him of what he had himself discovered at the start. Deeply self-critical, he would always cut and discard without regret. When we did *Measure for Measure* he was inspired by the name Angelo and spent long, secret hours with the wigmaker, preparing an angelic wig of shoulder-length blond locks. At the dress rehearsal no one was allowed to see him, until he came onto the stage, delighted at his new disguise. To his surprise, we all howled our disapproval. "Ah," he sighed, "Goodbye, my youth!" There were no regrets and the next day he made a triumph, appearing for the first time with a bald head.'

After the revival of the equally acclaimed *Much Ado*, the third production of 1950 was *Julius Caesar*, directed by Michael Langham and Anthony Quayle, who also played Mark Antony, with Andrew Cruickshank as Caesar, Harry Andrews as Brutus and Gielgud playing against his instinct as a hard-edged, embittered and knowing Cassius. 'The performance of the season,' J.C. Trewin called it, 'and – I would say – the Shakespearean performance of the year'.

Gielgud's final Stratford appearance that year was less sure-footed, at least at the opening. J.C. Trewin again: 'On the first night it seemed that Gielgud's King Lear had not grown since the Vic revival of 1940: until near the end the actor, intellectually commanding, illuminated the part from without rather than from within: he was slow in developing pathos, though once the premiere was over his grip on the part strengthened.'

Fortunately, one or two of the critics went twice and the Lear they saw the second time round displayed none of the initial uncertainties. According to T.C. Worsley, 'In the first we were conscious of Mr Gielgud acting: we admired the grasp, the range, the subtlety, the sureness, the intellectual force, the largeness. In the second . . . this seemed not acting – something conscious and willed – but the actual enacting itself of events seen for the first (and only) time, into the heart of which we ourselves are led, stumbling with the old king down the deep descent.'

All in all, it had been an extraordinary season for Gielgud, one, as Richard Findlater noted at the time, that 'had deepened and widened his acting range, ripening his fine sensibility, intelligence and skill', and one that had given him renewed confidence in his powers and a new awareness of his inner strengths and potential.

With the exception of *Julius Caesar*, which the public had enjoyed, but with which he and the company claimed to have been ill-at-ease, Gielgud had found the season satisfying as well as stimulating. He had particularly enjoyed working with the *wunderkind*, Peter Brook – 'He was awfully clever at knowing when I was false. One wants to be told when one is bad and false, but one doesn't want to be put down so that one loses confidence' – and renewed his association with him the following year when he played Leontes in Brook's Festival of Britain production of *The Winter's Tale*. Gielgud sensed that Leontes might offer him similar opportunities to those he had exploited so effectively as Angelo.

Leontes and Angelo are not evil figures bereft of all moral sense (unlike Iago, which Gielgud never played, or Ferdinand in *The Duchess of Malfi*, which he did not enjoy), but real people with all the failings and frailties of humanity. To Gielgud the parts offered not only opportunities for creating subtle psychological portraits, but also effective theatre: 'Angelo and Leontes . . . are both given wonderful scenes of repentance in which they are shamed, humiliated and at last forgiven. These later scenes give a fine opportunity for the actor to show both sides of the character.' Gielgud took that opportunity and enjoyed another success that confirmed that, at forty-seven, he was again at the height of his considerable powers. After visiting the Edinburgh Festival, *The Winter's Tale* moved to the Phoenix for a record-breaking run, where Gielgud followed it up with the revival of *Much Ado*. Next he returned to Stratford to direct Ralph Richardson in an unhappy production of *Macbeth* (Kenneth Tynan was 'unmoved to the point of paralysis' and, unfortunately, was not alone) before flying off to Hollywood to recreate his Cassius in Joseph Mankiewicz's film of *Julius Caesar*.

It was around this time that Tynan had his first meeting with Gielgud. On 22 March 1952, the young critic wrote to Cecil Beaton: 'John G, whom I'd never met, asked me suddenly to supper, and we talked until three, I coaxed into silence by his beauty, he garrulous and fluttering as a dove. What a possession for any theatre! It is irrelevant to say that he was fair in this part, good in that, brilliant in that: Gielgud is more important than the sum of his parts, and any theatre that has him securely lashed to its mast will not steer dreadfully wrongly.'

Gielgud returned to London in the autumn of 1952 with plans for a season of three plays to be presented by the H.M. Tennent management at the Lyric Theatre, Hammersmith. *Vogue* magazine was among those that looked forward to the event with relish: 'John Gielgud, the nonpareil, the cynosure of the theatre, is the flashing, sparkling mind behind this new season of such infinite promise – he will direct three plays, acts himself in the second and third. Now his powers are at their greatest – sensibility, strength, imagination, wit, combined to make the true aristocrat of both tragedy and comedy.'

Richard II was to be the opening production and Gielgud had contemplated returning to the role himself, but resisted the temptation, feeling he would now be thought too old for the part. He gave it instead to Paul Scofield who had just turned thirty and who made a success of it under Gielgud's direction, despite the difficulty of working with a director who clearly still felt the part to be his own.

The Lyric season's second offering was Congreve's *The Way of the World*. A few critics cavilled at Pamela Brown's Millament, but most agreed with Kenneth Tynan that Gielgud had produced a sparkling revival: 'Having assembled what I heard described, in an enviable slip of the tongue, as "a conglamouration of stars," he has let them have their heads. The play sails into life with pennants flying. Mr Gielgud is at the helm, a crowd of deft character actors like Eric Porter, Richard Wordsworth, and Brewster Mason are manning the rigging, and Eileen Herlie is thrown in for ballast. To pipe us aboard there is Paul Scofield as Witwould, the amateur fop – a beautifully gaudy performance, pitched somewhere between Hermione Gingold and Stan Laurel. Gielgud's galleon would not be complete without a figurehead, and there, astride the prow, she triumphantly is – Margaret Rutherford, got up as Lady Wishfort, the man-hungry pythoness.'

The surprise of the Hammersmith season was Thomas Otway's *Venice Preserv'd*, regarded by many as the finest post-Jacobean tragedy and popular with leading actors from the time it was written in 1681 to the early nineteenth century, though little performed since. Gielgud hadn't seen the last major revival – in 1920, also at the Lyric, Hammersmith – but he had read the play more than once and was confident it had potential. Peter Brook's production realised that potential and *Venice Preserv'd*, with Gielgud and Scofield well matched in the two leading roles, was the critical success of the season – albeit the only play to lose money.

It was during the run of *Venice Preserv'd* – and thanks, in part, to personal representations made to the Prime Minister, Winston Churchill, by Laurence Olivier and Ralph Richardson, both of whom had been knighted in 1947 – that, in Queen Elizabeth's Coronation Honours List, Gielgud received the recognition that so many of his colleagues and his public felt was long overdue.

'I have a special memory of the magnificent JG,' Paul Scofield told me recently. 'It was 1953, during his season at the old Lyric, Hammersmith, that John received his knighthood. We were playing Otway's *Venice Preserv'd* in a superb production by Peter Brook. John's first entrance was followed by a long solo speech. On the night that the news of the knighthood broke, John's entrance was greeted by a huge, roaring ovation. It went on and on. I have never heard anything like it. He waited silently, and waited – the tears streaming down his face. This I observed from the wings, my own entrance being at the end of his speech. Finally, the uproar subsided and he spoke. He was by then completely in control of his emotion, except for that tear-drenched face. His soliloquy ended, I came on stage and our subsequent scene was exactly as always, except for my own rather shaken sensation of having been on the spot and having witnessed, at close quarters, a piece of theatre history.'

It was the best of times, it was the worst of times. For Sir John Gielgud, 1953 turned out to be a year of honour – and humiliation. That summer in Bulawayo, as part of the Rhodes Centenary Festival (organised by his former lover and lifelong friend, John Perry), Gielgud bade a final farewell to one of his most cherished roles. At forty-nine, he had wanted to play Richard II one last time, but quickly realised it was a serious mistake. 'I was terribly disappointed to find that, contrary to my expectations, it gave me no joy at all. I could only imitate the performance I saw when I was a young man. And I thought, "No, I must leave this part alone because the fact that I am older and wiser doesn't make me better in the part. I just give an imitation of what I used to do and I did it better then because I was young." You can't imitate a young part with any pleasure.'

While he played it with great effect, there was not much real pleasure to be had from Gielgud's next role, that of the humourless, fastidious prig Julian Anson in N.C. Hunter's *A Day by the Sea*. Gielgud had wanted to do a new play and had the option of the Hunter piece or of taking on John Whiting's much more complex and challenging *Marching*

Song. Gielgud, encouraged by Binkie Beaumont, went for the safer, softer option, and appeared with an all-star cast – Ralph Richardson, Sybil Thorndike, Lewis Casson, Irene Worth, Megs Jenkins – in what Tynan described as 'an evening of unexampled triviality', which (as it turned out) was exactly what the public seemed to want.

It was at the end of a long day's rehearsal for *A Day by the Sea* that Gielgud allowed himself what he immediately realised was 'an evening of unexampled stupidity'. On the night of Tuesday 20 October 1953 the great actor, newly knighted, was arrested for soliciting in a public lavatory in Chelsea. He was taken to Chelsea police station where he gave his name as 'Arthur Gielgud of 16 Cowley Street, Westminster' and described himself as 'a clerk earning £1,000 a year.' He was charged with importuning and ordered to appear at Chelsea magistrates' court the following morning where he pleaded guilty, apologised humbly to the resident magistrate – 'I cannot imagine how I could have been so stupid. I was tired and had had a few drinks. I was not responsible for my action' – and was given the standard fine for the offence: £10.

The magistrate, E.R. Guest, did not appear to be aware of the defendant's celebrity. 'I hear something like six hundred of these cases every year,' he said, 'and I begin to think that they ought to be sent to prison . . . I suppose on this occasion I can treat you as a bad case of drunk and disorderly and fine you accordingly . . . See your doctor the moment you leave here and tell him what you have done. If he has any advice to offer take it, because this conduct is dangerous to other men, particularly young men, and is a scourge in this neighbourhood.'

Overnight, Gielgud, distraught, had contemplated suicide. What he feared most was the effect on his mother, now eighty-five. 'I thought it might kill her. She hated publicity of any kind. Thank God my father had died before that because he would never have got over it.' In the event, he decided to face the music and did so alone. Before the hearing, the only person in whom he confided was his GP, a Dr Woodcock, from whom he borrowed the money to pay the fine.

Gielgud's arrest and appearance in court might well have gone unnoticed by the wider world had not a reporter from the *Evening Standard*, on his way to cover another case, chanced to be in the building early that morning and recognised the famous Gielgud voice and profile. By lunchtime, Sir John's misfortune was front page news.

Amazingly, overnight Gielgud did not consult Binkie Beaumont, his closest professional ally, the producer of *A Day by the Sea* and a notorious 'Mr Fix-it' who might – just might – have been able to persuade the police to let their victim off with a caution and drop the charge. Beaumont's biographer, the actor Richard Huggett, described what happened when rehearsals resumed on that fateful Wednesday: 'When the company assembled for the afternoon rehearsal they all knew and when Gielgud returned they were all there and waiting for him. A heavy silence fell and a terrible embarrassment gripped them, for nothing like this had ever happened to them and there were no guide-lines for the correct social behaviour. Should they ignore it as if it had never happened? Should they offer condolences? Or should they make light-hearted, perhaps jokey, references to it? It was Sybil Thorndike who knew just what to say. She punctured the balloon of tension and embarrassment with a carefully timed and chosen tactless remark. She rushed across the rehearsal room, embraced him, kissed him on both cheeks and said, loudly and laughingly, "Oh, John, darling, you have been a silly bugger."'

That evening, according to Huggett, there was a meeting at Beaumont's house with all the Tennent hierachy and their legal advisers. 'What was to be done? Gielgud offered to give up the part and to retire from the theatre until the scandal had died down, but Binkie wouldn't let him. If he didn't face the public in this play then he would never be able to act again and he could retire permanently if that was what he wanted.' It was agreed that the proposed tour – Liverpool, Edinburgh, Manchester – followed by the opening at the Theatre Royal, Haymarket, would go ahead as planned.

In a letter written to their son later that week (on 24 October, Sybil Thorndike's seventy-first birthday), her husband (and fellow cast member) Lewis Casson said: 'Our excitement about the new play has been terribly complicated by this unfortunate Gielgud business. I think Sybil has told you something of it. Rather foolishly he took on the job of producing and playing a very long part. Got very strained and tired – and there you are . . . We were all in fits as to what would happen, but Tennents and he decided to go on. But we don't know yet what the results will be either when we produce in Liverpool or still more in London. Personally I think it's quite likely to be to some extent a plant by the authorities.† It's all a great pity.'

In his biography of his parents, John Casson reported that 'their fears of disaster for the new play proved to be, if not

† On the night of his arrest Gielgud may indeed have been 'entrapped' by the police. The public lavatory in question was known to be used by homosexuals for 'cottaging' and was under police surveillance.

groundless, at least unjustified. But this was mainly thanks to Lewis and, even more, to Sybil, who had the larger part in the show. Lewis told me later that when she made her entrance on to the stage at Liverpool she fixed the audience with a look as though she were saying, "I don't think it matters. Do any of you?" and daring them to think otherwise. Apparently nobody dared.'

Richard Huggett, in his biography of Beaumont, gives a somewhat richer account of that memorable opening night: 'Gielgud's first entrance as Julian Anson, the diplomat, was a quarter of an hour into the first act, probably the longest and most crucifying fifteen minutes of his life. When the moment came he could not enter: he was paralysed and shaking with fear. Once again it was Sybil Thorndike who came to his rescue. She was on the stage having just completed a short scene with Irene Worth. When Gielgud didn't appear she could see him in the wings, knew what was the trouble and what had to be done. She walked off through the french windows, grabbed him and whispered fiercely, "Come on, John darling, *they won't boo me*," and led him firmly on to the stage. To everybody's astonishment and indescribable relief, the audience gave him a standing ovation. They cheered, they applauded, they shouted.'

I wasn't there, but I did know Richard Huggett a little and my instinct is that his description of the reception accorded to Gielgud that night may be a mite exaggerated. Certainly, the Liverpool audience was generous to Gielgud and the warmth of their welcome – and that of the London audience when the play opened at the Haymarket – moved him deeply and came as an enormous relief both to him and the Tennent management. *A Day by the Sea* was a considerable commercial success.

This was (to put it mildly) a difficult time for Gielgud personally – apart from anything else, his older brother Lewis had recently died – and a tiring time for him professionally. While appearing in *A Day by the Sea*, he directed first, a commercial pot-boiler in the form of *Charley's Aunt*, the Brandon Thomas farce in which he had first appeared exactly forty years before, and then, at the Lyric, Hammersmith, his own adaptation – designed to make the dialogue more naturalistic and colloquial – of *The Cherry Orchard* with Trevor Howard and Gwen Ffrangcon-Davies. The strain told on him, he began to suffer from double-vision, he had what we would now call 'a nervous breakdown' – though the Chekhov did not appear to suffer. Noel Coward went to see it and was entranced: 'A magical evening in the theatre; every part subtly and perfectly played, and a beautiful production so integrated and timed that the heart melted. We came away prancing on the toes and very proud that we belonged to the theatre.'

The Gielgud make-up included great resilience as well as vulnerability, and that resilience was needed in 1955 when, after directing a disappointing *Twelfth Night* at Stratford with the Oliviers (Sir Laurence as Malvolio, Vivien Leigh doubling as Viola and Sebastian), he took on King Lear in a production that was dominated – swamped even – by the work of the Japanese designer Isamu Noguchi. In the programme Gielgud explained that the object had been 'to find a setting and costumes which would be free of historical or decorative associations so that the timeless, universal and mythical quality of the story may be clear . . .' In the event for many critics and most spectators the background was both too bizarre and too obtrusive, though for more than a few 'the greatness of Sir John's interpretation was not altogether dimmed.'

Looking back on the 'great disaster' a decade later Gielgud was able to pinpoint where he felt he and his director had gone wrong: 'The great mistake I made in the Japanese *Lear* was a purely technical one. Noguchi, who is a sculptor, designed the sets and sent them to us and we thought they were thrilling and I still think they were, but I did not know at the time that he had never designed costumes. He arrived with no costumes, he designed them very hastily, he left before he had seen the fittings, he was not at the dress rehearsal or the first night. We all looked so strange and peculiar and I remember saying to George Devine who was directing the play: "Don't you think we could discard all the costumes and get some rubber sheets and make them into drapes and all wear sort of nondescript cloaks? I believe with this scenery that might work." And I still believe it might have done; but we hadn't the courage at the last moment to make such a drastic alteration, so I went through with it because I felt Noguchi was too individual and brilliant a designer to throw overboard completely, or half throw overboard which would be even more dishonest.'

The Japanese *Lear* – which, according to Gielgud, was admired by the young and the avant-garde and which Peter Brook acknowledged as the starting point for his own triumphant production of the same play with Paul Scofield eight years later – was coupled with the revival of *Much Ado about Nothing* and both played to packed houses in London and on two brief European tours.

From Shakespeare, Gielgud wanted to turn again to something modern and light. He settled on the part of the valet in Noel Coward's *Nude With Violin*. Coward had hoped for Rex Harrison and accepted Gielgud as an alternative with a little reluctance. In November 1955, Coward confided to his diary, 'Binkie is very keen for Johnny Gielgud to play *Nude with Violin* and so, although I do not think him ideal, I have consented. He is a star and a box-office draw, and although his comedy is a bit heavy-handed his quality will be valuable. Fortunately there is no love element and no emotion in the part, and if he plays it down, as I have implored him to do, he will probably, with a strong cast round him, make a success of it.' He did indeed. In general the notices were dire, and in particular Kenneth Tynan was at his most vitriolic ('Sir John never acts seriously in modern dress; it is the lounging attire in which he relaxes between classical bookings; and his present performance as a simpering valet is an act of boyish mischief, carried out with extreme elegance and the general aspect of a tight, smart, walking umbrella'),† but the public paid no attention and turned up at the Globe Theatre in droves.

Gielgud stayed in the play for nine months, only leaving when he was due to start rehearsals for Peter Brook's Stratford production of *The Tempest* in the summer of 1957. This time he conceived Prospero as a character in a revenge play, 'gradually being convinced that hatred and revenge are useless'. He played the role as a powerful but embittered aristocrat, with concentrated anger and anguish, 'his face all rigour and pain, his voice all cello and woodwind' (Tynan) and many regarded it as the definitive Prospero. When it transferred to London, it filled the vast Theatre Royal, Drury Lane, for sixty-one performances.

---

† In later years Gielgud would say, 'Tynan wrote I only had two gestures: the left hand up, the right hand up. What did he want me to do? Get my prick out?'

A year later Gielgud returned to Shakespeare and to the Old Vic for his first appearance in *Henry VIII*. Given his physique and timbre, he was unlikely casting for Cardinal Wolsey and, while the big scene that depicts the Cardinal's downfall – the moment that had drawn Gielgud to the play – was played with poignancy (and Gielgud tears), the Tynan verdict was endorsed by many: 'Though Sir John made good use of his poker back and doorknob face, he never for a moment suggested Wolsey the self-made "butcher's cur"; all was rigid declamation, issuing from a tense and meagre tenor.'

His return to Stratford and his next untried Shakespeare was even less successful. *Othello*, directed by Franco Zeffirelli with Sir John as the Moor, Ian Bannen as Iago, Dorothy Tutin as Desdemona and Peggy Ashcroft as Emilia, fell victim to one of those disastrous first nights – complete with cumbersome costumes, shaky scenery and half-remembered lines – that are sometimes entertaining to hear about, but always agony to endure. While several of Gielgud's colleagues and one or two of the critics sensed the potential of a great performance, the production was reckoned a failure. 'This was a bitter blow to me,' he confessed a year or two later, 'because I've wanted all my life to play Othello, although I'm quite sure the public would never think me a satisfactory Othello in every way because I haven't got what Agate used to call the thew and sinew.'

Though utterly charmed by Zeffirelli as a man, Gielgud's confidence in him as a director never became established: 'Zeffirelli made the fatal mistake of dressing me as a Venetian, so that I looked, as many of the notices said, like an Indian Civil Servant. I didn't stand out from the others. Desdemona was over-dressed, I was under-dressed, there was much too much scenery, there were, I think, very damaging cuts, and certain other members of the cast were to my mind fatal. And it was terribly badly lit, which was very strange for Zeffirelli. He had dark scenery, so that with my dark face and dark clothes people couldn't see me – and when one feels one is not well lit, one is immediately at a disadvantage. He also did some terribly dangerous things, like putting me far too much upstage; he had a wonderful-looking scene with a huge table and imprisoned me behind it so I couldn't get any contact with the audience or with the other actors.'

However, Gielgud was to enjoy a Shakespearean success at this time, not in any play, but in his one-man show based on George Rylands' Shakespeare anthology, *The Ages of Man*. The solo recital was given its first public showing at the Edinburgh Festival in September 1957, followed by a brief European tour. A year later Sir John took it on a more extensive tour of Canada and the United States and then on to Broadway, where it won great acclaim. Even the sometimes grudging Kenneth Tynan, while repeating his line that 'Gielgud is the finest actor on earth from the neck up,' conceded that it was one of the 'most satisfactory things' Sir John had ever done: 'Poker-backed he may be; poker-faced he certainly isn't. Wherever pride, scorn, compassion, and the more cerebral kinds of agony are called for, his features respond promptly, and memorably.' Not everyone found the solo recital so satisfying – 'He was superb in his quiet moments, but not so good when he wept and roared' said Coward – but it provided Sir John with a perfect vehicle for his unique vocal virtuosity and he was to perform it, off and on, around the world for several years to come.

In 1958, shortly before he set off for the first American tour of *The Ages of Man*, his mother died at the age of eighty-nine. A couple of years later, in an interview he gave in New York, he talked about the solo recital and the way the use of personal images had helped him in performance: 'When my mother died two years ago – I had never seen anyone dead before – it naturally made a tremendous impression upon me, and at a certain moment when I was doing the recital which came soon afterwards, in the "To be or not to be" speech, on a certain line, I always thought of her, of exactly how she looked when she was dead. It came into my mind, it didn't hold me up, but it gave me exactly the right feeling of the voice for the line. It came to me naturally, you know, without knowing it the first time, and it was so vivid that I thought I could never speak the speech again without thinking of it, because it would help me to make the line right, and it always did.'

seven

'YOU'VE ALREADY SHOWN ME THAT – NOW SHOW ME SOMETHING ELSE'

1958–1968

For ten years, between 1957 and 1967, John Gielgud performed *The Ages of Man* around the globe, from Ireland to the Soviet Union, from the West End to Broadway. As a solo performer of Shakespeare he enjoyed an enviable success wherever he went. As an actor, over the same period, his fortunes were more mixed.

In 1961 he returned to one of his great loves, Chekhov, and received warm praise for his endearing, self-mocking portrayal of Gaev in *The Cherry Orchard*. This was a Royal Shakespeare Company production, directed by Michel Saint-Denis, with Peggy Ashcroft as Madame Ranevsky, and almost as long a rehearsal period as they had enjoyed when the three of them had last worked together on *The Three Sisters* in 1938. *The Cherry Orchard* did not achieve the same extraordinary success, but Gielgud found his part 'delightfully rewarding'; it 'suited me, I think, better than any other in which Saint-Denis has directed me; at least I enjoyed working for him more on this occasion than ever before.'

The actress Constance Cummings has a special memory of the production: 'When I think of John's performances, the one moment that always comes to my mind first is a small, quiet moment in Act II of *The Cherry Orchard*, as Gaev stands apart, fingering a small wallet absently, and says to no one in particular, "I have been offered a job in a bank – 6,000 roubles a year." You could *hear* him thinking, "What an absurd idea . . . that trip to town was really useless . . . what should I do in a bank . . . that's not going to save the orchard . . . me in a bank . . . good God . . ." How did he do it? All he said was, "I have been offered a job in a bank." How did he spin this magic?'

Gielgud turned again to Chekhov in 1965, when he directed and played the title role in the commercial West End premiere of *Ivanov*. He had admired the play ever since he had seen it – his first Chekhov – directed by Komisarjevsky in 1925. Gielgud gave it a thoughtful and loving production that many critics found uneven and some found laboured. The cast included Yvonne Mitchell as Anna Petrovna, Claire Bloom as Sasha and Roland Culver as Lebedyev. Culver's verdict on Gielgud as a colleague on stage is typical: 'John is a delightful and completely unselfish actor to work with. I had a long, rather charming scene with him in the third act, which I enjoyed immensely. I had several lengthy speeches to which he listened as attentively as I did to his. Listening in the theatre is as important as talking.'

On tour and in London it was not unsuccessful. One night, an improbable member of the audience was Roland Culver's friend, Bing Crosby: 'He had never seen a Chekhov play before and did not expect to enjoy it, but his wife had insisted on taking him to see us. He had, he said, thoroughly enjoyed every moment and asked me to congratulate the cast.' In 1966, when the production transferred to the United States, with Vivien Leigh replacing Yvonne Mitchell, Crosby's compatriots were less enthusiastic. The press was so-so and business was poor, but, according to Culver at least, Gielgud enjoyed the experience: 'We arrived in New York in February and had several weeks' rehearsals with the new cast, so John had lots of fun directing the new boys and girls, and leading them round the mulberry bush.' The pre-Broadway tour took in Washington DC, Philadelphia, Boston and Toronto, where the company's hotel caught fire: John appeared in vest and shorts. 'What's the matter?' he asked.

'The hotel's on fire, John.'

'Ah,' said John, 'I'm not surprised. I thought I could smell burning. Perhaps I'd better get dressed . . . I really think it would be quite sensible to make a graceful exit. I don't think I like the idea of being carried down a fire escape on a fireman's back!'

Much more solidly successful on both sides of the Atlantic was Gielgud's revival of Sheridan's *The School for Scandal* in 1962. With a starry cast – Ralph Richardson, Margaret Rutherford, John Neville, Daniel Massey, Anna Massey – he directed the play with predictable polish at the Theatre Royal, Haymarket, and then took over from John Neville as Joseph Surface before the whole production moved to Canada and the United States where it played to excellent business and enthusiastic notices. Gielgud's Joseph Surface was considered the 'very model' of how the part should be played: stylish, incisive, perfectly timed, impeccably phrased.

Geraldine McEwan, who took over as Lady Teazle for the American tour, told me she thought 'John was just perfect in his part – and I can't complain about his direction either. At the end of the second day of rehearsals, he came up to me and I was convinced he was going to give me a whole string of terrifying notes. He just looked at me with his bright, shining, twinkling eyes, rubbed his hands and cooed at me, "Oh, Geraldine, I do love acting with you!" I walked out into the street on cloud nine.'

The triumphs, however, were matched by disasters, and these all seemed to be in new plays. Gielgud hadn't yet discovered the knack – or simply had the luck – of finding original work by contemporary writers that both appealed to the public and suited his temperament and talent. In Graham Greene's *The Potting Shed*, as the overwrought James Callifer, a traumatised figure from Greene's gallery of whisky priests, Gielgud had several moving moments (when he was able to shed real Terry tears), but he was ill-at-ease in the play and, with exceptions, the critics found both the piece and the performance unconvincing.

In 1960, at the Phoenix, Gielgud and Richardson teamed up to appear in Enid Bagnold's latest offering, *The Last Joke*. This time the critics were derisive, the audience jeered and the run was brief. Jerome Kilty's dramatisation of Thornton Wilder's *The Ides of March* at the Haymarket in 1963 – with Sir John as Julius Caesar togged up in a lounge suit and shortie toga to create an uncomfortable ancient-cum-modern dress – was given a similar critical mauling. Again the audience booed. In Edward Albee's play *Tiny Alice*, on Broadway, at the end of 1964, audiences and critics were both bewildered and frustrated. Noel Coward saw it and reported to his diary: 'The first act was hopeful, after that a chaotic mess of sex and symbolism. Beautifully directed and acted except for poor Johnny G who was strained and unconvincing. Altogether a maddening evening in the theatre, so nearly good and yet so bloody pretentious.'

This was a bitter disappointment to Gielgud who yearned for a success in a contemporary play (the kind of success Olivier had scored at the Royal Court in John Osborne's *The Entertainer* and Ionesco's *Rhinoceros*) and he battled heroically to make the Albee work. The film critic Stanley Kauffman saw *Tiny Alice* and gave a chilling account of Sir John's lone struggle against the odds in the closing minutes of the play: 'Through the evening Gielgud and his colleagues had done their best with this spurious work but had progressively lost the audience. Then he was left alone – deserted, one could say – to finish, in a torrent of fevered rhetoric, a play that had long ceased to matter. The audience began to murmur and rustle as he kept on and on. The buzz swelled a bit, punctuated by giggles. Toward the end he seemed isolated, separated by an invisible wall of protest. I was filled with admiration, not because of any "show must go on" hokum but at his power of concentration, his inner ear. He had kept his own music going against a hostile chorus.'

Gielgud could have made a film of *Hamlet* in the 1930s. He was given the opportunity and offered the backing. He wasn't interested. He couldn't see it. In the 1940s and 1950s, of course, Olivier made films of *Hamlet*, *Henry V* and *Richard III*. In the run-up to the Second World War, Gielgud was the undisputed leader of his profession, the acclaimed classical actor of his generation. In the years immediately after the war, that mantle was transferred to Olivier's shoulders.

Gielgud was an indefatigable director, but, unlike Olivier, he wasn't a natural impresario, showman, producer. In 1952 Gielgud said, 'In some ways it might be pleasant to become an actor-manager, to be host in one's own theatre, with a permanent company and a settled policy – some ideal five-year plan of classic repertory alternating with modern work – and, of course, I have often hoped for this. But the financial organisation of such a scheme is an added burden. I have no talent for it, and in actual practice I dread the responsibility of committing myself for more than a few months ahead, lest my own enthusiasm wane before I have completed my task, and so bring the whole project to disaster.' Olivier had no such scruples: in 1962 he was appointed as first director of Britain's long-awaited National Theatre.

On 15 October 1965, Kenneth Tynan, who had given up his role as the *Observer*'s theatre critic to become the National's 'literary manager', sent a memo to his boss:

Dear Larry,

. . . I have a marvellous idea. People keep telling me that John G is dying to work with us. Why not ask him to play Robespierre with you as Danton with somebody else directing? I have a further suggestion. Why don't you alternate Lear and Gloucester with him? This would have enormous historical impact because of the *Romeo and Juliet* interchange [in 1935], and I needn't tell you what the box-office impact would be. I haven't spoken to John about this but pressures from many quarters suggest that he would be sympathetic to some such plan.

JOHN GIELGUD · An Actor's Life

Neither of these exciting ideas materialised and when Gielgud did come to make his debut with the National Theatre, in the 1967/8 season, the plays in which he appeared failed to catch the public imagination. As Orgon in Tyrone Guthrie's production of Molière's *Tartuffe*, Sir John was the victim both of improbable casting and of an uneven production that never seemed to get the balance of the piece quite right. And, again, with Ted Hughes' version of Seneca's *Oedipus*, directed by Peter Brook, while Gielgud gave what Olivier described as 'a perfect tragic performance', it was in the uncertain context of a controversial production that some found austere and unremitting and others awkward and eccentric. (The production is chiefly remembered for the setting, central to which was a gigantic golden obelisk. When she saw it, the Australian actress Coral Browne drawled, 'Well, it's nobody I know.' Late in rehearsals, Irene Worth, playing Jocasta, found she was positioned behind the obelisk and needed to be above it. 'Maybe we should raise it,' she suggested, 'Maybe we should put it on a plinth.' Gielgud emerged from the wings: 'Plinth Philip or Plinth Charles?')

Peter Brook agreed to direct this *Oedipus* for the National Theatre 'uniquely for the pleasure of working with John again after many years, although in the meantime my own way of approaching theatre had greatly changed. Instead of starting with a first reading, I now spent a long period doing exercises, largely involving bodily movement. In the company, there were a number of young actors very eager to work in this way and there were also several older actors for whom all these methods seemed dangerous new fads. The young actors angrily despised the older actors in return and, to my horror, they regarded John as a symbol of a theatre they had rejected.'

On the first day of rehearsals, Brook suggested the company start their work with some exercises demanding considerable physical involvement. 'We sat in a circle and the actors tried the exercise one by one. When John's turn came, there was a moment of tension. What would he do? The older actors hoped he would refuse. John knew that after the confident young actors he could only appear ridiculous. But as always, his reaction was immediate. He plunged in. He tried, he tried humbly, clumsily, with all he could bring. He was no longer the star, a superior being. He was quite simply there, struggling with his body, as the others would be later with their words, with an intensity and sincerity that were his own. In a matter of seconds, his relation with the group was transformed. It was no longer the name nor the reputation of Gielgud that mattered. Everyone present had glimpsed the real John; he had bridged the generation gap and from that moment he was held in true admiration and respect.'

Despite magnificent moments – the director Tony Richardson saw Gielgud in the Brook production and described the scene leading to the blinding of Oedipus as 'a moment of acting in all its richest imaginative and physical complexity as great as any I've ever seen' – these were not the best of years for Gielgud the actor, nor even for Gielgud the director.

Throughout his career, other than at the start and at the finish, when he was not performing in a play Gielgud was directing one. From his first production of *Romeo and Juliet* for the OUDS in 1932 ('fresh and clean' Harcourt Williams had called it) to his last West End offering in 1975 (a disappointing revival of Pinero's *The Gay Lord Quex*), Gielgud was responsible for more than sixty productions and the range of work was immense: Shakespeare, Chekhov, the classics, flimsy potboilers, quality revivals, worthy middle-of-the-road commercial plays suitable for 'canopy names' to star in, even grand opera – at Covent Garden in 1957 he directed the first English professional stage performance of Berlioz's *The Trojans*;† in 1961, again at Covent Garden, with Solti conducting and spellbinding designs by John Piper, he produced the first London performance of Benjamin Britten's *A Midsummer Night's Dream*;‡ and in 1968 he was responsible for the *Don Giovanni* at the London Coliseum.

With so much work over so many years, inevitably the quality was variable, but from start to finish Gielgud the director was known for one besetting sin: the constant changeability of his quicksilver mind. In 1938, writing about Gielgud as both actor and director, Michel Saint-Denis observed, 'When one sees Gielgud, it does not take long to discover that he is

---

† The actress Dulcie Gray told me of the rehearsal she attended when the Trojan horse appeared on stage for the first time and Sir John attempted to get the chorus to respond with suitable displays of amazement and terror. The singers' acting abilities disappointed the director. 'No, no, no,' he cried, 'That won't do at all. You look as if you're seeing not very good friends off from Waterloo.'

‡ In *The Many Faces of Gielgud*, Sir Georg Solti recounts a moment from rehearsals: 'I was at the piano, while Gielgud was instructing the boy playing Puck. Failing to make a particular point, Gielgud said, "Look, watch me – I'll show you how I want it." With that this elegant British gentleman, in his immaculate suit and shoes, stepped on to the makeshift platform. Suddenly we heard the voice of a gleeful adolescent and there before us stood the cheeky and glorious boy Puck.'

restless, anxious, nervous and impressionable. He is not over-confident in himself. His restlessness goes with a tendency to be dissatisfied. Therefore he works out more and more plans, more and more ideas, rejecting one for another, working all the time from instinct rather than from careful study.'

When Wendy Hiller was first directed by Gielgud (in 1944, in *The Cradle Song* by Gregorio Martinez Sierra), at the dress rehearsal, he suddenly called for hush: 'Be quiet everyone. I'm in a frenzy.' 'Frenzy' seems to have been a state all too familiar to both director and cast in Gielgud productions. In any memoir of what it was like working with Gielgud the director, complaints about his restless quest for something new and different come up again and again. At the start of rehearsals the incessant changes could be stimulating and inventive: as the first night neared they became alarming. Cecil Beaton on *Lady Windermere's Fan* in 1945: '*Lady Windermere* has opened to excellent notices on its trial trip to the provinces. All portends well: it has been a comparatively smooth undertaking. Few major alterations have had to be made although until the last minute John Gielgud continued to change his direction.'

Laurence Olivier recalling *Twelfth Night* in 1955: 'He still had the disconcerting habit of changing moves at every single rehearsal; of course a director has the right to change his mind, but after almost four weeks and with the opening night looming closer, I began to be nervous that the occasion would be a shambles, with an utterly confused company knowing neither the timing nor the placing of the moves. Noel Coward once said that the only real use of a director was to stop the actors from bumping into each other; at the rate our *Twelfth Night* was going our first performance would have been more like a game of Blind Man's Buff than anything else.'

Coward himself on *Nude with Violin* in 1956: 'John has directed the play with loving care and reverence and given everyone so much fussy business to do that most of the comedy lines are lost. They get up, sit down, carry trays in and out, change places and move around so incessantly that I nearly went out of my mind . . . It is extraordinary that a fine director like Johnny, who can do *The Cherry Orchard* and *A Day by the Sea* so superbly, should have gone so very far wrong. I can only conclude that it was over-anxiety.'

Roland Culver on *Five Finger Exercise* in 1958: 'Gielgud has the happy knack of getting the best out of his cast, but I should warn any young actor who may be privileged to be directed by him not to mark the stage moves on the script in ink, as at the end of a couple of weeks' rehearsals, each page might well resemble a pattern of tangled knitting, John being a little hazy for some time as to where on the stage the actor should be at any given moment . . . John's method, of course, takes a lot of the monotony out of rehearsals, each day is an adventure and one is kept on one's toes.'

The 1955 Stratford production of *Twelfth Night* featuring the Oliviers is famous for several archetypal Gielgud stories. One has Gielgud telephoning Olivier in the middle of the night with yet another bright idea.

'Larry, I've had a thought. I think you should play Malvolio very, very fat.'

Olivier, woken from a profound sleep, bleated, 'John, it's two o'clock in the morning!'

'Oh, very well then,' said Gielgud, 'Very, very thin!'

With forty-eight hours to go before the opening, the cast pleaded with Gielgud to be allowed one run-through of the play without interruption. 'We beg you, John,' said Olivier, 'We've

King Lear, with Stephen Haggard as the Fool, Old Vic, 1940. (*Mander & Mitchenson Theatre Collection*)

Macbeth, Piccadilly Theatre, 1942. (*Mander & Mitchenson Theatre Collection*)

For his performance in *Arthur*, 1981, with Dudley Moore and Liza Minelli, Gielgud won an Oscar. (*Orion/courtesy Kobal*)

Ralph Richardson, Laurence Olivier and John Gielgud, sharing a scene together for the first time (at the combined age of 233) in Tony Palmer's film, *Wagner*, 1983. (*Kobal*)

On the stage of the Old Vic at the party to mark his eightieth birthday, April 1984. (*Author's collection*)

Prospero, aged eighty-six, in Peter Greenaway's film, *Prospero's Books*, 1990. (*Allarts/Camera 1/ Cinea/courtesy Kobal*)

had all this chopping and changing. We can't take any more. Let us just run the play through once and see how it goes.'

'Of course, Larry, you're quite right,' said Gielgud, humbly. 'I shall sit at the back of the stalls and be as quiet as a church mouse. You won't hear a peep out of me, I promise. We'll take the play right from the top and I shan't say a word. On my honour.'

Much relieved, the company took up their opening positions and, with a deep breath, Orsino began: 'If music be the food of love –'

From the back of the stalls came a cry from the most famous fluting voice in British theatre: 'Oh, no, no, no, no, no!'

After the first night, Gielgud called the cast together to give them notes. Vivien Leigh said, more in sorrow than in anger, 'Everyone knows what we've been through, John, and after this I don't think anyone in the profession will want to work with you again.'

Gielgud looked up: 'Edith Evans might . . . at a pinch.'

Much of Gielgud's work as a director after the war – from *The Heiress* with Peggy Ashcroft and Ralph Richardson in 1949, when he was brought in at the last minute and performed a radical rescue job, to a pleasing *Private Lives* with Maggie Smith and Robert Stephens in 1972† – was successful: clear-cut, well orchestrated and stylish. Some of

---

† It was a rehearsal for this production that inspired another famous Gielgud gaffe. Maggie Smith, playing Amanda in *Private Lives*, had recently starred in the film, *Travels with My Aunt*. Directing the Coward play from the stalls, Gielgud interrupted a scene to give his leading lady a note: 'Oh, don't do it like that, Maggie, don't screw up your face. You look like that terrible old woman you played in that dreadful film . . . Oh no, I don't mean *Travels with My Aunt*.'

the productions were too busy, fussy and confused – Terence Rattigan's relatively effective *Variations on a Theme* (1958) was one, M.J. Farrell and John Perry's disastrous *Dazzling Prospect* (1961) another – but many more – *The Chalk Garden* (1956), *Five Finger Exercise* (1958), *Half Way Up the Tree* (1967) – were the reliable work of a seasoned craftsman.

In 1963 Gielgud defined the qualities he regarded as essential to a Shakespearean director: '. . . industry, patience . . . sensitivity, originality without freakishness, a fastidious ear and eye, some respect for, and knowledge of, tradition, a feeling for music and pictures, colour and design; yet in none of these, I believe, should he be too opinionated in his views and tastes. For a theatrical production, at every stage of its preparation, is always changing, unpredictable in its moods and crises.'

A year later he directed his own last Shakespearean production: *Hamlet* on Broadway with Richard Burton. The reviews were mixed, but the receipts were fabulous and the production ran for 138 performances, breaking Gielgud's own record by six performances. The Burton–Gielgud collaboration attracted a mass of publicity, a ton of newsprint and at least two full-length blow-by-blow accounts of the making of the production. In one, William Redfield, the actor playing Guildenstern, revealed that he and others in the cast were alarmed to find that Gielgud as a director didn't concern himself with 'the play's circumstances but only with its effects'. Gielgud quoted his old mentor Harley Granville-Barker to them in an attempt to encourage them to pace, shape and colour their performance rather than relying exclusively on circumstance and absolute psychological truth: 'Granville-Barker once said to me,

"You've already shown me that – now show me something else." It was a wonderful direction for me because I tend to be monotonous. After that, I always made sure that each scene I played had a different colour, a new shape. Even the lines should change every few moments or so. If I do one line this way, then the next should be that way and then the next should change and the next. It's good to keep the audience off-balance, you know – always interested – perhaps even a bit confused.'

Gielgud did not feel that the non-British members of the *Hamlet* company were convinced by his approach. 'The American cast did not appear to understand very much of what I was trying to do. All they wanted was motivation. I was attacked after every rehearsal by desperate actors asking "What is this character *about?*" I fear that, in the end, my ill-tempered reply would be, "It's about being a good feed for Hamlet."'

Naturally, he confessed, with actors of the first rank his approach was less didactic: 'If I direct a play with wonderful actors, I know that my work will not be as difficult or will not be the same as when I get an ordinary cast of fairly good actors. I mean, if you get Peggy Ashcroft and Edith Evans, as I had in *The Chalk Garden*, I say that I just put up the tennis net and clear the court and act as referee, because they know much more about what they want to do than I do. I'm only there as a kind of audience to check the spacing, the movement, the pace of the play. You can't really direct people who are enormously talented, I don't think.'

But you can try. The only time Gielgud and Richardson had any serious difference of opinion in a production was when Sir John was directing Sir Ralph in *The School for*

Scandal and they couldn't agree over Richardson's first crucial entrance as Sir Peter Teazle. 'Ralph argued every day and we could not begin to rehearse the scene. "Should I have a newspaper in my hand? A walking stick? Or be taking snuff perhaps?" At last one morning he leaned across the footlights and said, "You know, Johnny, I prayed to God last night to tell me how to come on in this opening scene. And this morning God answered, 'Do what it says in the text, just come on.'"'

Much of Gielgud's best work as a director was in plays in which he appeared himself. Being both director and star is a risky combination: 'People are always saying they think it's not a good plan; my most intimate friends have always counselled me against it, and thought I took on too much. There's no doubt that I did overtax my strength very often.'

One of the great advantages of a director being in his own production, of course, is that he is there at every performance: 'After the play has opened, if I've only directed it, I come back every six or eight weeks to see it, and I find things have slipped and gone wrong, and I go back and see the actors and they're very hurt. They say, "Oh, we've been working very hard, while you were sitting at home drawing the money, and why should you tick us off, we've made this pause and it's so effective, and we get a big laugh on this line." If you complain about these things they take it rather badly and it's hard to make them rehearse well. But if you're in the play yourself, you can, two or three times a week, send little notes down, or you can rehearse a little bit before the play begins, or a little bit after, or you can go over something yourself, or you can talk to the person you're acting a scene with.'

The real danger of the director-star role in Gielgud's case was that too often he would concentrate on the production as a whole to the detriment of his personal performance. He gave his first energies to the rest of the company, leaving a full consideration of his own role till last: 'When I go on the road before we come to London, I get all the players as good as I can, and I put my own part in really as a sketch: it's rather hard on the audience, and perhaps on the actors too. But I keep on making my understudy walk for me, and when we've been on the road for a few weeks, I have another rehearsal and I make the understudy walk my whole part. I remember this worked extremely well, particularly in *The Lady's Not for Burning*, *Ivanov*, and *Much Ado*, and certainly in *Love for Love*, because I was able, after a few weeks, to see exactly where my part belonged in the pattern, and drop into it to complete the picture, like the missing piece of a jigsaw puzzle.'

eight

'NEW NOTES FROM AN OLD CELLO'
1968–1994

In 1955 Peter Hall's production of Samuel Beckett's *Waiting for Godot* at the Arts Theatre in London marked the beginning of a new dramatic era. The heyday of the proscenium arch was coming to an end; the golden age of Noel Coward and Terence Rattigan, of Frederick Lonsdale and Enid Bagnold, of 'well-made plays', cast to the hilt and impeccably packaged by the all-powerful Binkie Beaumont, was drawing to a close. 'New writing', 'Kitchen sink drama', 'The Theatre of the Absurd' were set to have their moment in the sun.

In 1955 Sir John Gielgud was invited to appear in *Waiting for Godot* (as were Ralph Richardson, Alec Guinness and other established luminaries) but declined. In 1958 – when the success of *Godot* was worldwide and John Osborne's *Look Back in Anger* and Harold Pinter's *The Birthday Party* were the talk of the town – Gielgud was asked to play in the British premiere of Samuel Beckett's *Endgame*. He turned the offer down: 'I couldn't find anything that I liked in the play.

I thought it's no good pretending for pretension's sake that I would play this play, because it nauseates me. I hate it and I won't play it, and yet I long to be in something as avant-garde as that.'

As the fifties gave way to the sixties, Gielgud began to regret the way he had publicly expressed his lack of sympathy with the new writers, began to envy an actor like Olivier who had risked going to the Royal Court and playing in Osborne and Ionesco, began to feel that he was becoming 'old hat' while being unsure of what could be done about it.

This sense of being out of touch, unable to relate to the writers of his time, lasted for several frustrating and unnerving years, until in 1968, at the age of sixty-four, he accepted the part of the Headmaster in Alan Bennett's play-cum-revue *Forty Years On*, and gave a witty, assured, self-mocking performance that was to earn him his best notices in a decade. *Forty Years On* was hardly 'cutting edge': it was a nostalgic pastiche – yet it was the vehicle that brought Gielgud back into the vanguard, that suddenly made him seem in no way a man out of his time but rather the complete contemporary.

As well as writing the piece, Alan Bennett appeared in it and kept a diary of the experience† that offers a wonderful portrait of Gielgud at the time:

24 May 1968. [Supper to meet Gielgud.] He is taller, squarer than he seems on stage. I am very nervous, knowing that if it comes to 'selling' the play I won't be able to say much. Not to worry, as Gielgud talks all the time, telling story after story, head back on the sofa, famous

† Published in *Writing Home*, Faber & Faber, 1994.

nose in profile . . . He is currently appearing at the National in Peter Brook's production of *Oedipus*, which I don't let on having seen. Stories are rife of the indignities to which the actors have been subjected . . . Gielgud is very loyal to Brook over all this, saying simply that, while it has been hard going, he is sure the difficulty and embarrassment of it have done him good.

2 September. . . . In the morning the plotting goes ahead slowly, with Gielgud sitting apart doing his eternal crossword. I have heard stories that he is apt to fill in any old word that is the right length. I sneak a look and am disappointed to find this is a myth.† He learns his script by writing it out in a neat hand on the page opposite the text. 'I am a very bad study. After fifty, one gets much worse.'

He is full of ideas for his own part and for the play, many of them good, some cock-eyed. The cock-eyed ones take a lot of getting rid of. He is quite frank about this, saying that when he directs he always warns the actors he will come up with a dozen ideas, only one of which will be of any help. . . . 'I think I should speak to the audience,' he had said at the first reading. 'I am very good at that. I like singling people out.' 'I can't bear speaking to the audience,' he says this afternoon. 'And it's so old hat, singling people out. I can't bear that.'

---

† The actor David Dodimead told me he had once been sitting next to Sir John while both of them were separately attempting *The Times* crossword. Dodimead marvelled at the speed with which Sir John was rattling through the clues. He looked over Gielgud's copy of the newspaper and queried one particular word that the great actor had just filled in. Dodimead said, 'Sir John, what on earth are "Diddybums"?' 'I've no idea,' said Gielgud, happily, 'But it does fit awfully well.'

30 October. Noel Coward comes to the final preview. After the performance . . . I sit in my room hoping Coward has liked it and that if he hasn't he'll have the tact not to show it. Any criticism or even advice at this late date is destructive. And I remember the story of Gielgud rehearsing a speech in an empty theatre, the only other person there a charwoman mopping the stage. At the finish she is reputed to have leaned on her mop and said, 'I don't think you should do it like that, dear.' 'Really? Oh God, how do you think I should do it?' John G sends Mac [his dresser] to fetch me in to meet Coward, who is brimming with enthusiasm and saying all the right things.

10 November. In the first week the play has broken all box-office records and is an assured success. Gielgud is very happy and in wonderful form.

Over the next ten years Gielgud took on a whole series of demanding roles by new and 'difficult' writers and did so with an apparent confidence and ease that would have suggested to someone who had not known of his career before the late 1960s that here was an actor who was a natural frontiersman. The parts themselves were varied: Sir Gordon Petrie, the Bertrand Russell figure in Peter Shaffer's word-blown *The Battle of the Shrivings*; Harry, one of the patients in the mental home in David Storey's elliptical masterpiece, *Home*; Sir Geoffrey Kendle, an hilarious carica-ture of Gielgud himself, in *Veterans*, Charles Wood's comedy born out of his experience as scriptwriter for the film of *The Charge of the Light Brigade* in which Sir John had played Lord Raglan; Shakespeare in despairing and embittered old age in

Edward Bond's *Bingo*; Spooner, the down-at-heel Bohemian writer *manqué* in Harold Pinter's elusive *tour de force No Man's Land*; Sir Noel Cunliffe, the elderly acidic archaeologist in Julian Mitchell's morbid *Half-Life*.

These were all uncompromising pieces of their time – and three of them were presented at the Royal Court, a theatre at which Gielgud would have felt sadly out of place a decade before. Several also involved the use of language that – in the words of John Mills, Gielgud's co-star in *Veterans* – 'was definitely not for the ears of Auntie Mabel or the grandchildren'. Before *Veterans* opened at the Royal Court in March 1972, the play went on a pre-London tour, taking in Edinburgh, Nottingham and Brighton. According to Mills, in Edinburgh the piece was received in 'shocked and stony silence': 'John and I got letters from the public telling us we should be ashamed of ourselves. Someone even sent me a ten bob note saying I must be pretty hard up to have to appear in filth like this. But there was worse to come. In Brighton, a man in the circle, sitting not far from Mary, my wife, was so outraged he got up and addressed the rest of the audience. He said, "This is the last time I come to the theatre. These actors are a disgrace to their profession. I have never heard such disgusting language in all my life." He marched out of the theatre and, as he was going, Mary distinctly heard him mutter, "And I paid good money to see them two fuckers."'

In between playing the 'moderns', Gielgud did not altogether neglect the classics. He played Julius Caesar twice: at the Chichester Festival Theatre for Robin Phillips in a stylised and uneven production of Shaw's *Caesar and Cleopatra*, and at the National Theatre for John Schlesinger in

Shakespeare's *Julius Caesar*. At the National he also worked with Peter Hall. They had been acquainted since the '50s – and Hall, as founder-director of the Royal Shakespeare Company, had offered to redirect the failed Zeffirelli *Othello* at Stratford in 1961 – but they hadn't worked together until *The Battle of the Shrivings* in 1970. Now they became close colleagues and Hall's diaries of the period are full of delightful insights to Gielgud's character. In 1977, Sir John played Sir Politick Would-be in Ben Jonson's *Volpone*. The production was lack-lustre, but Gielgud's eccentric performance endearing. During one rehearsal Hall mentioned something about the dangers of over-playing. Gielgud blushed: 'Will I never learn? Still my old tricks after years and years and years: anything for a laugh, and because of that I don't get it.'

Gielgud's tendency to come up with a dozen ideas a minute – many of them mutually contradictory – was undiminished too. In *The Tempest*, in 1973, Hall planned to present the play as a masque with Gielgud's Prospero dressed up in the style of the Elizabethan wizard Dr John Dee. Gielgud had his doubts. 'JG began the afternoon by announcing that he didn't want to wear a beard or hat or be in grey or black as Prospero, who was a boring man, and it was a boring part, and he didn't want to look boring. He questioned practically everything that I proposed . . . JG remembered that when he first played *The Tempest*, it was all divinely Eastern and he wore a turban. In a later production, he recalled, he wore a long grey beard and glasses. Then in Peter Brook's he had some kind of ragged, hermity shift with sandals. At the end of three hours, I had gently but firmly ridden John to a standstill and managed to get him to listen to why I was doing the play in a Jacobean masque-like way.

He then announced that he loved the set, and perhaps he had better wear a buttoned, belted, scholar's coat after all. And a beard (should he grow it or have a false one?). And he agreed to wear a scholar's hat. JG runs around in circles with huge charm and energy. He keeps making self-deprecating remarks, reminding us we shouldn't listen to him, and that he is a romantic who loves the old-fashioned theatre.'

Though he retained reservations about his costume – and some about the production as a whole – Gielgud trusted and admired Hall. Judging from Hall's diaries the feeling was mutual: 'He is an amazing man, and my debt to him is enormous. He has never complained, never been restless. He has led the company and helped me every inch of the way.'

It was in Hall's production of Harold Pinter's play *No Man's Land* that Gielgud enjoyed the outstanding success of his seventies. Once again his stage partner was his colleague and friend of fifty years standing, Ralph Richardson. When Lindsay Anderson brought them together as the two elderly mental hospital inmates in David Storey's *Home*, they had already played together on many occasions, but their work together now, in the Indian summer of their careers, seemed to have a magical dimension that their earlier stage encounters had lacked. As an American critic said, 'they simply make beautiful music together'. In *Home* it was in many ways the greater challenge for Gielgud since he had less to say, less to hold on to and work with. He had to ring the changes of colour, shape, tone, feeling, from a minimum of words, brief interjections, spasmodic sentences that trailed away, silences, but he did so with consummate technical expertise and breathtaking emotional force. Keith Dewhurst described the performance in the *Guardian*: 'Gielgud's weeping is a depth of emotion which he must find entirely within himself, since in the sense of story-line or interaction between the characters there is very little in the play to help him . . . In *Home* the character just interrupts a conversation with tears and the way in which Gielgud does this, the way in which his whole face goes red and his eyes blink with salt, is simply an act of genius: a consummation of his lifetime's integrity.'

The success of *No Man's Land* – at the National, in the West End, on Broadway, on television – was prodigious. The moment Gielgud read the play he had known he wanted to do it. 'Peter Hall had sent the script to me expecting that I would want to play the "posh" part of Hirst, because it was more the kind of role I had done in the past. I told him "Don't be silly. The other part is infinitely more what I want to play." The part of Spooner was a complete impersonation, such as I had never had a chance to do in the theatre. It was very exciting to have a chance of doing it, and I was quick in finding a way to look and to dress. The moment I read the play I saw Spooner clearly, which was rare for me. I remember saying to Harold Pinter, "I think Auden, don't you? Do you think sandals and socks?" and he jumped at the idea. Then I said, "Do you think we should add spectacles?" and he liked that too. About a week after we started rehearsal I came on the stage with a wig, the suit and the spectacles and everybody said, "It's exactly right, perfect!" and I said, "Yes, and now I must find a performance to go inside it."'

The performance he found – wry, sly, at some moments ingratiating, at others vulnerable – was perfectly matched by Richardson's: they were a couple of masterly virtuosos at the

height of their power. What the play was about – the no
man's land between illusion and reality, between half-truth
and self-awareness – was in many ways neither here nor
there. As Gielgud said: 'Why should the play "mean"
anything if the audience was held the whole time and was
never bored?'

Gielgud's farewell to the stage came ten years later in 1987,
when, at the age of eighty-three, he appeared in Hugh
Whitemore's *The Best of Friends*, an elegant evocation of the
epistolary relationship between Sir Sydney Cockerell, the
Director of the Fitzwilliam Museum (JG), Bernard Shaw (Ray
McAnally) and the saintly Abbess of Stanbrook Abbey
(Rosemary Harris). The director of the piece was James Roose-
Evans and he recalls how Gielgud, having agreed to play the
part within thirty-six hours of reading the script, then had
second thoughts: 'Our producer, Michael Redington, Hugh
Whitemore and I drove down to Sir John's stately pavilion in
Buckinghamshire, only to be greeted by a change of mind.
"I'll gladly do it on radio, but really don't see how it will work
on stage." Michael Redington, knowing that I had resolved this
challenge, now said, "Jimmie, tell Sir John how you see the
play being staged." And so, scene by scene, I went through the
play, Gielgud becoming gradually more excited so that when
we were joined for tea by his friend Martin Hensler, he said,
"Jimmie, tell Martin how you see the play."

'Having agreed to do the play Sir John was nonetheless, as
he wrote to the publisher John Murray, "very apprehensive
at the responsibility of acting in the theatre again after so
many years." This apprehension remained throughout the
run. Each night before the performance, he would sit on
stage, quietly waiting for the play to begin, looking drawn

and anxious. And each night, at the curtain call, he would look years younger, like a boy in love. He had done it again! Conscious of his age, he always relished the last line of the play which became a delicate joke shared with his audience: "The angel of death seems quite to have forgotten me. On the other hand, I might pop off tomorrow. Who knows?"

'Although he had learned the part in advance, rehearsals were a daily torture to him as he suffered momentary blackouts, and each time he dried in his frustration he would stamp the floor fiercely with one foot.

'On the first day of rehearsals, I worked on the first scene with him and then suggested we go back to it. "No, no," was his response, "I'd like to go on. I want to see what happens next." And so we continued, scene by scene, until by the end of the third day the whole play had been blocked, and he smiled with relief, realising that the play was going to work and not just be, as he had feared, a recital piece. It was the only time I have ever blocked a play so swiftly, and is not my usual procedure, but it was clear that he needed the reassurance of the overall *mise-en-scène*. On good days his own invention would flow swiftly, almost in one "take".

'In his first night note to me he wrote, "I hope you will continue to correct my faults and to be on the look-out for any small improvements I may hope to make." Often at dinner, after a performance, he would remark, "Did you notice how I phrased that line tonight? I think it works better like that, don't you?" Throughout the run he never ceased to hone a performance through which, as Michael Billington observed, shone an essential nobility of spirit.'

As his stage career began to wind down, Gielgud's television and film career was starting to take off. In 1983, under the banner headline 'New Notes from an Old Cello', *Time* magazine ran a two-page spread on the phenomenon of the English actor who, in his eightieth year, had become 'the hottest young talent around':

Question: Is it possible to make a movie or TV series without John Gielgud?

Answer: Yes. But it is not easy.

Since 1980 his face has been on more screens than the MGM lion. Famous to serious theatregoers for more than 50 years, the reserved, sometimes frosty-appearing Gielgud has, in his 70s, suddenly assumed a new role – that of Major Movie Star.

Gielgud made his film debut in the 1920s in a couple of silent pictures: the first, a French melodrama, *Who is the Man?* (originally written as a stage piece for Sarah Bernhardt), in which he played a neurotic sculptor and morphine addict; the second, an Edgar Wallace thriller, *The Clue of the New Pin*, in which he was cast as the villain, 'frantically disguised in a long black cloak, black wig, spectacles and false teeth, and always photographed from the back'.

He made his first talkie in 1932, and then only appeared three times on the screen – without much pleasure or acclaim – before making his Hollywood debut in 1952 in Joseph L. Mankiewicz's celebrated *Julius Caesar* with Marlon Brando and James Mason. Gielgud's portrayal of Cassius was a success. Juxtaposed with Gielgud, Mason later admitted, 'I felt depressingly feeble, particularly in the vocal department. He spoke with such richness and authority and was charged with such emotion, while I who had been mumbling my way through one movie after another, now had a voice which was deplorably lacking in mobility and range.' Gielgud, of course, was helped by the fact that he had already played the part on the stage. Inevitably, he had to reduce the scale of the performance he had given in the theatre: 'I couldn't make the faces or give the shouts, and it was quite a different feeling. But I was much more in control of the part because I knew the whole line of it, each scene, even if there were cuts or scenes shot out of sequence.'

He returned to Shakespeare on the screen as Clarence in Olivier's electric *Richard III* in 1955, as Henry IV in Orson Welles' flawed but still fascinating adventures-of-Sir-John-Falstaff compilation, *Chimes at Midnight*, in 1966, and as Caesar himself in Stuart Burge's pedestrian version for television in 1969. For many years Gielgud found film work unsatisfactory and unsatisfying: he did not like the early starts, and found it difficult to give a cohesive shape and flow to his performance given the way pictures are shot piecemeal and rarely in chronological sequence. When *Chimes at Midnight* was first shown, a friend told him that one of his most effective moments in the film came shortly after Hotspur's death when Gielgud looked first at Falstaff, next to Hotspur's body and then at Prince Hal – 'but we never did the scene at all. On the last day Orson said, "There's a close-up I have to do of you, just look down there, that's Hotspur's body, now look up at me." I never even saw Orson made up as Falstaff, but it appears that, because of the clever cutting, this scene of glances between four people is enormously effective. That shows how much you owe to the cutter and the director when it comes to the screen. You can't really control your own performance at all.'

Keith Baxter, however, who played Prince Hal in *Chimes at Midnight*, believes that the experience of working with Orson Welles marked the beginning of a new attitude from Gielgud towards the movies: 'I believe it was the first time Gielgud allowed himself to be persuaded that he actually had something very exciting to offer the cinema. Now that we have become accustomed to seeing many fine Gielgud performances on the screen, it is difficult to believe that there was a time when he lacked confidence before the camera. Over the years he had convinced himself that his style was not suited to the screen.'

Welles, according to Baxter, encouraged Gielgud 'to use his imagination as freely as he might if he had been playing Henry IV in the theatre. This was a tremendous psychological release to Gielgud, who chattered away with suggestions to Welles all the time. It was not a question of whether Welles used Gielgud's ideas that mattered – sometimes he did not, but sometimes he did – it was the fact that Gielgud's creative juices had not been fully stimulated until then. Welles knew that Gielgud's innate taste and instinct would discipline his talent and that he would adapt his performance to the less familiar medium. Nothing was more moving than seeing these two extraordinary men working in tandem so happily together, laughing unrestrainedly, so full of respect for each other, especially after they had both been so nervous of not coming up to each other's expectations. No wonder that Gielgud, in his letter to me from New York, wrote: "Oh! I do miss Orson's brilliance and all the fun!"'

In 1954, Gielgud had been one of the forty-four guest stars Mike Todd persuaded to make cameo appearances in *Around the World in Eighty Days*. In 1956 the need to clear some surtax got the better of his judgement and he appeared as an overpowering and perverse Moulton Barrett in a dire remake of *The Barretts of Wimpole Street*. In the same year he played the Earl of Warwick in Otto Preminger's laborious version of *Saint Joan*, with the ill-starred Jean Seberg. In 1963 he was cast as the French king Louis VII in the glossy Richard Burton/Peter O'Toole *Becket*, and earned himself an Oscar nomination. In 1964 he was one of the redeeming features of Tony Richardson's disappointing film of the Evelyn Waugh satire on the American way of death, *The Loved One*. By the time he worked for Richardson again in 1967 in *The Charge of the Light Brigade* his film career was beginning to gather momentum.

The many pictures in which he appeared during the final thirty years of his life were of vastly varying quality. He must be the only theatrical knight to date to have appeared in pornography, the notorious Bob Guccione enterprise *Caligula*: 'They offered me the part of the Emperor Tiberius, and I turned it down, saying, "This is pure pornography." Gore Vidal, who wrote the original script, then wrote me a terrifically rude letter, saying how impertinent it was of me to refuse it and that if I knew what Tennessee Williams and Edward Albee said about me, I wouldn't be so grand. Terrible vituperation. Then they offered me another smaller part that wasn't dirty, and I rather shamefacedly took it. I played a whole scene in a bath of tepid water. It took three days to shoot and every two hours some terrible hags dragged me out, rubbed me down and put me back into the water again. Most extraordinary proceedings.'

In several of the better of the films he took on in the 1970s and '80s – *The Elephant Man, Murder on the Orient Express, Chariots of Fire*, for example – and in a number of the more memorable television productions in which he was involved – notably John Mortimer's award-winning adaptation of Evelyn Waugh's *Brideshead Revisited* – Gielgud gave beautifully telling cameo performances, but in only one or two did he have roles of sufficient size and scope to reveal him as a screen actor of the first magnitude. In 1976, working with David Mercer's script in Alain Resnais' film *Providence*, his performance was a revelation. 'Gielgud is superb,' Peter Hall wrote at the time. 'Not only is his acting subtle and rich but his feelings are so great, his passion is so enormous, that he suggests heterosexuality in a way I would never have believed possible for him.' And Stanley Kauffman, the doyen of American film criticism, writing in *The New Republic*, was overwhelmed by his extraordinary vocal technique: 'What shading, what music – and never for its own sake. Everything he says is placed as if by divine order, the phrasing and pitch illuminating what he and the words are about. His lines here are studded with profanities, and in the mouth of this devilishly gleeful, highly articulate character, every one of them made me laugh. And to see him, ruddy-cheeked, bald-pated, big-nosed, treating each moment of life left to him like one more gob of pâté or gulp of wine, commenting on his pain like a spectator at a predictable black comedy – what a pleasure. What a *pleasure*.'

Kauffman first saw Gielgud on the screen in *The Good Companions* in 1933 and, having watched him over the years in films and on stage, relished the development he felt privileged to have been able to witness. To look back on Gielgud's career gave him considerable delight: 'Part of the pleasure I get in that retrospect is in what he has done with himself technically: how what I first heard as a vibrant, somewhat too pressing voice has become a confident, easy instrument, greatly expanded in compass and greatly enriched in the quality of each note within that compass; how his movement, which had once included an often-parodied, heavy, almost pigeon-toed walk, was now smoothed and burnished at least to fit his needs without distraction. Part of my pleasure is in the fact that he is older and, as all interesting human beings do, has grown larger through living. And much of the pleasure is in the patent evidence that, unlike so many gifted people, particularly gifted Americans, he has grown by living like an artist. I know nothing of his private life other than public rumour, and I don't care; I know something of the poor choices he has made in his career. Still he has become proof, irrefutable, that he thought of his life in relation to artistic purpose – with art as his centripetal force, his map, his reason for getting through each day and wanting to get up again next morning. Only an artist who gets serious joy out of shaping his life to nourish his art can finish like Gielgud.'

In 1982, exactly fifty years after making his first talking picture, John Gielgud was awarded his first Oscar. He won the Academy Award for Best Supporting Actor for the role of Hobson, valet, confidant and surrogate father to playboy millionaire Dudley Moore in *Arthur*. It was a witty, knowing, wicked performance in an otherwise flawed film, but whether or not it was really his greatest screen performance is irrelevant: in Hollywood terms, it was his finest hour.

By his own lights, Gielgud's finest hour in the cinema is more likely to have been his last assault on Prospero in Peter

Greenaway's highly individual (and visually sumptuous) adaptation of *The Tempest*, released in 1990. According to Greenaway, the notion of the film came from Sir John: 'Gielgud had played Prospero many times and had more than once considered committing the role to film.† A particular wish of mine was to take the maximum advantage of his powerful and authoritative ability to speak text – verse and prose – so that, as well as playing Prospero, he was persuaded to voice, for the most part, the dialogue of all the other characters in the drama as well.

'Prospero, omnipotent magician, inventor and manipulator of characters, can be conceivably appreciated as a Shakespearean self-portrait. Prospero is the last major role that Shakespeare invented, reputedly, in the last complete play he wrote, and there is much, both in the character and in the play, that can be understood as a leave-taking of the theatre and a farewell to role-playing and the manufacturing of illusion through words – not insignificant perhaps when Gielgud's seventy-year career on the stage is considered.'

And for most of those seventy years, John Gielgud was reckoned a 'star' – whatever that may mean. If you asked Sir John himself what qualities defined a 'star' performer, he produced an interesting list: 'Energy, an athletic voice, a well-graced manner, certainty of execution, some unusually fascinating originality of temperament. Vitality, certainly, and an ability to convey an impression of beauty or ugliness

---

† 'I have always wanted to make a film of Prospero,' Gielgud said in an interview in 1978. 'Prospero has been a favourite part of mine and it would be a wonderful thing to do at the end of one's career, because it is so obviously Shakespeare's last work – the end of his career.'

as the part demands, as well as authority and a sense of style.'

I gave that list to Kenneth Branagh at the time he was directing and starring in his own film of *Hamlet* (in which Gielgud made a fleeting guest appearance) and asked Branagh if he felt it summed up Gielgud's own qualities as an actor. 'John also conveys great intelligence,' he said, 'a mind at work. He can present Hamlet as a man of feeling and as a man of thought. John is a formidable intellect, whatever he may say to the contrary.'

As well as directing a radio production of *King Lear* to mark Sir John's ninetieth birthday, Branagh also worked with him on a short film of Chekhov's *Swan Song*. 'John always brings complete commitment to his work. With *Swan Song*, we rehearsed for a day, one week in advance of our schedule. The piece was 22 minutes long and mainly a monologue for John, but even at rehearsals he knew it by heart. And he was funny. Not bad at eighty-eight! His other great gift is humility, the genuine kind. He's never too grand to take a note from a director, even a much younger one, and when he gives a note (as he sometimes has to me during our radio adventures) he does it with real grace and generosity.'

Through his many films, through his numerous television appearances (in the United States, even through his commercials for Californian 'champagne'), in the final thirty years of his career John Gielgud won himself a vast new audience, an audience, of course, that, as likely as not, had never seen him in his true setting: the theatre. He once admitted that he had never understood politics or world affairs. 'I am lacking in ambition for power, large sums of money, or a passionate desire to convince other people that they are wrong and I am right,' he said. 'But I have a violent and sincere wish to be a good craftsman, and to understand what I try to do in the theatre, so as to be able to convince the people I work with.'

The theatre was what he knew best and loved most in life; it was, without exaggeration, what he lived for. Once, when asked to talk about his proudest achievement, he replied: 'One thing I'm proud about in my career is the influence I've had on other actors who worked in my company, before the war particularly, and the general influence I've had in the theatre, because I am a very timid, shy, cowardly man out of it. But once I go into a theatre, I have great authority and I get great respect and love from all the people working in it – from the stagehands, the costumiers, the scene designers and the actors – and this suddenly justifies your entire existence. I think that it is something that is much more precious to me than any personal success that I have had as an actor.'

—— nine ——

'THE END OF AN ERA'
1994–2000

I first heard that Sir John Gielgud had died on Friday 9 April 1999. At lunchtime I received a call from the editor of the *Sunday Telegraph* breaking the sad news and asking for a 3,000-word appreciation of the great actor's life by 6.00 pm, 'seven o'clock at the absolute latest'. I took the telephone off the hook, put the metaphorical damp towel around my head and set to work. At 6.30 pm I called the editor's office to plead for an extension to the deadline. I was then told that all afternoon the office had been trying to get hold of me to put me out of my misery. The news of Sir John's death had been premature. No one was quite sure how the rumour had started, but Sir John's agent had spoken to him in person during the day and could report, categorically, that his client was alive and well and looking forward to his ninety-fifth birthday the following week.

I had believed the false report of Sir John's death so immediately, not only because, at his great age, death at any time was a possibility (and I knew that recently he had been in hospital having taken a tumble and hurt his leg), but principally because, only a few weeks before, his friend and companion of nearly forty years, Martin Hensler, had died of cancer.

For the last fifteen months of his life, John Gielgud lived alone. He lived in style and comfort, of course, he was well looked after, but he was both lonely and sad. The actress Dulcie Gray, who had known him for many years† and lived nearby on the outskirts of Amersham, saw quite a bit of him during his final year. 'Johnny was heartbroken when Martin died,' she told me. 'They had been together a very long time and he missed him dreadfully. Some people had reservations about Martin, but I liked him awfully. I met him first, years ago, at a party given by Laurie Evans.‡ He was standing on his own, looking rather lonely and I went and talked to him and liked him at once. I think that was one of the reasons Johnny liked coming to see me. He knew that I'd always been fond of Martin. Yes, Johnny was getting frail. When he came for lunch before Christmas he was all right, but when he came in January he was on sticks and he didn't like that much. He had always been so erect, you know, so proud of his wonderful posture, so full of style. And when he came for the last time he was on crutches and his driver had to help move him from chair to chair. It was sad to see and he hated it, but he coped. It was a nuisance and it bothered him, but the real blow had been losing Martin. Martin dying like that broke his spirit, broke his heart.'

† They met when Gielgud directed her in *Landslide* at the Westminster Theatre in 1943.
‡ Laurence Evans, agent to Sir John, Laurence Olivier, Ralph Richardson and a raft of other leading actors of their generation.

During his final year Sir John mourned the loss of his friend and fretted about the lack of work. In London, a little joke went round theatrical circles: 'John G is thinking about changing his agent. He's not getting offered the right kind of parts.' At South Pavilion, Sir John, in his ninety-sixth year, gainfully employed through eight decades, was anxious, unhappy, not amused. His niece, Maina Gielgud,† daughter of Sir John's elder brother Lewis, remembered her uncle towards the end: 'Always when I saw him, or when we just spoke on the telephone, he'd say, "I just wish there would be some work. They have all forgotten me." He was just waiting, waiting for the phone to ring.'

Maina has no children and is almost the last of the line. The great Terry-Gielgud dynasty has dwindled to her, another nephew and a great-niece. Her father and Sir John's other brother Val (who became head of BBC Radio Drama) died years ago and their younger sister Eleanor (who was Sir John's secretary for some years after the war) died at the beginning of 1999. Mrs Gielgud had died in 1958, in her ninetieth year. Her husband had died eight years before. Maina remembers, as a girl, Christmas day visits to Sir John and Martin Hensler at 16 Cowley Street: 'I was the only child there. It wasn't a family Christmas – only a dozen theatrical people. Martin always brought in a pile of telephone directories for me to sit on; one fewer every year until I was tall enough to reach the table.

'I always got on very well with Martin. He was very eccentric. He had these strange animals – exotic birds in

---

† Former ballerina and sometime artistic director of Australian Ballet. When she was nine, Sir John summoned her to his dressing room: 'Do you really want to dance? Oh, Maina, acting would be so much easier.'

cages in the lavatory, and iguanas. He was very nice to me, but some people didn't like him. Perhaps they were protective of their own friendships with John. But John needed Martin, just as Martin needed him. I do not know what drove it – devotion, familiarity or love – but it was a terribly important relationship in both their lives.'

When Sir John died, *The Times* published two fascinating articles by the writer Julie Kavanagh, who was befriended by Gielgud during the last three years of his life. Kavanagh's memoir included an intriguing glimpse of the Gielgud-Hensler relationship: 'April 14, 1998: Gielgud's 94th birthday at South Pavilion, his house in Buckinghamshire. Four of us are having lunch at a long Regency table laden with crystal and silver – or rather three, as Martin Hensler, his partner of 35 years, sits at a slight distance in his usual place, his chair against the wall. He does not eat or drink – he cannot stomach much besides bread and black coffee, a legacy of his impoverished Hungarian past, he says – but talks animatedly in a gutteral accent, his long Rothman's Royal spilling ash onto his knees. . . . I realised later that I had been invited to the birthday celebration as a kind of buffer as relations between Martin and Paul [Anstee, a friend of Gielgud's since the 1950s], a former lover, had always been strained: "Martin took against me on principle." Looking like a retired accountant with heavy spectacles and thick, toupée-textured black hair, Martin was tolerated rather than liked by Gielgud's friends, most of whom resented his emphatic opinions, unremitting nagging, or worse. . . . Martin was a mystery to everyone, Gielgud included. "He won't speak about his early life at all. I do know that he had a terrible time in Hungary. Obviously they had great estates and palaces and parks and things. I'm fascinated but I know he hates talking about it so I never urge him to do so. If people speak Hungarian to him he won't answer."...

'Martin, a friend remarked, "is an extraordinary mixture of total commitment and fury. Fury at being committed. He could no more leave John than fly." The dependence was mutual. For Gielgud, life without Martin would have been "Oh, hopeless – I wouldn't know what to do", while Martin said more than once that when Gielgud died, he was going to shoot the dogs and then shoot himself.'

During his final year, Gielgud was bereft ('I can't get over Martin. I never thought he'd die. I was sure I'd go before him') and found neither comfort nor satisfaction in looking back over his lifetime's achievement. His fretfulness included a nagging anxiety about his 'failure to make a proper contribution' during the Second World War. More than once he told me, 'I feel very guilty that throughout the war I was able to carry on working in the theatre. I was quite fit. I could have served in uniform, but I didn't.' He claimed that, at the time, he had no idea that, behind the scenes, Binkie Beaumont had pulled strings to ensure that his star player was available to entertain the troops rather than serve with them. 'I learnt about it years later through Kitty Black. It is very shaming.'

When, in 1996, he joined the Order of Merit, he played down the honour, brushing references to it aside, almost brusquely. Famously, when his agent called to congratulate him, he said, 'Never mind that – what news of the part?' Despite Gielgud's growing sense that he had been forgotten, in fact he went on being offered – and accepting – work well into his nineties. In January 1997, when he was approaching ninety-three, he collected a raft of superlative notices for his appearance in *Shine*, a film based on the true story of a gifted musician, David Helfgott, in which Gielgud, playing the part of Cecil Parkes, a partially paralysed Royal College of Music professor, turned a cameo into a fully-developed performance that, for many critics, was the making of the picture. In April 1999, just before his ninety-fifth birthday, he appeared around the world in a high-budget (if none too memorable) television film, *Merlin*. The casting director for the movie was Noel Davis: 'The producers wanted Sir John in the picture because he was a star name, a name that was good to have on the credits – and on the box of the video. And with Gielgud, of course, as well as a name and a reputation, you got real class. He was also quite delightful to work with. His rate was £50,000 per day, but he guaranteed you a second day free. He was clear about his hours – 10.00 am to 12 noon and then 2.00 pm to 4.00 pm – and you had to supply him with a helper, someone assigned exclusively to him, to look after him, take him from make-up to the set and so on. But he wasn't grand. He didn't require a car. He got his regular driver from the local taxi firm in Aylesbury to bring him in and take him home.' His final film engagement came not long before his death, a small part in a Samuel Beckett piece, *Catastrophe*. It was work, but Sir John was not happy: 'They haven't given me any lines.'

Gielgud's work in the cinema and for television in the last three decades of his life, combined with his income from the commercials he made for Paul Masson wines in the United States, ensured that he died a wealthy man. One newspaper estimated his final fortune at £10 million. When he was younger, he had had no head for figures, nor much interest in the detail of domestic finance. At the beginning of the Second

World War, when Binkie Beaumont suggested to Kitty Black that her duties might include providing Gielgud with secretarial assistance, 'I was horrified to discover,' she said, 'he had no savings account and, determining that he would never feature in a bankruptcy proceeding, made him open a deposit account from which he would have funds to pay his income tax.'

John Gielgud died, wealthy, honoured and admired, on Sunday 21 May 2000. Vincent, who helped Sir John in the house and garden, called Maina Gielgud with the news: 'He said that Uncle John had passed away just after lunch. That it had been very quick and totally peaceful. He had just got up from his seat and stumbled. John was ninety-six. And still it is hard to imagine he has gone.'

Gielgud's death was reported on front pages around the world. Buckingham Palace issued a statement saying, 'The Queen has learned of his death with sorrow.' The lights were dimmed outside every West End theatre in tribute and Dame Maggie Smith echoed the thoughts of many when she said, 'We shall not see his like again. It is the end of an era.'

The obituarists, after the false alarm in 1999, were ready with their tributes. 'Fastidious performer with a matchless voice, who stood centre stage through the whole history of modern British theatre', ran the headline in *The Times*. 'Sir John Gielgud was an actor who, more than any other, enshrined the spirit of English classicism. . . . To a unique degree his greatest performances coincided with the greatest plays. "Style," he once said, "is knowing what sort of play you're in." And to those who saw him as Hamlet, Mirabell, or John Worthing, the experience was not simply that of witnessing a wonderful performer making the most of a wonderful part: it was to be in brain-to-brain contact with

Shakespeare, Congreve and Wilde. As with Kean and Irving, his art was partly one of physical transformation. He entered the theatre during the epoch of the matinee idol and was able to assume romantic good looks in spite of a large nose, rapidly thinning hair, and legs that gave him acute embarrassment. What was never in doubt was the quality of his voice: an instrument of spell-binding purity, unrivalled in its speed and sensitivity of articulation.'

The *Daily Telegraph* obituary began: 'Sir John Gielgud, who has died aged 96, was challenged only by Laurence Olivier for the title of greatest English actor of the twentieth century.' On the front page, the paper reported that the agent Laurence Evans, who had represented both Gielgud and Olivier (as well as Richardson), had no doubt: Gielgud was the greatest of them all.

Olivier's achievement was certainly colossal. His range was extraordinary, his versatility immense. He had an animal magnetism and a physical energy that Gielgud lacked. Olivier won himself a worldwide audience by becoming a film star in the 1940s when Gielgud was still fighting shy of the cinema. Gielgud declined to commit his Hamlet to film and dismissed the idea of putting *The Importance of Being Earnest* on the screen,† while Olivier

---

† Dulcie Gray told me that her late husband Michael Denison, then under contract to Associated British Films, had alerted the company to the fact that *The Importance* would come out of copyright in 1950. The Denisons took Gielgud to dinner at The Ivy to persuade him to direct the film of the play. 'Oh, no,' said Gielgud, 'I don't think so. I've been doing the play for years and years. I don't see it as a film, do you? Of course, it might be rather fun to do it in Chinese.' When the film was made, it was directed by Anthony Asquith, with Michael Redgrave in Gielgud's role as John Worthing, and Michael Denison as Algernon Moncrieff.

made films of *Henry V*, *Hamlet* and *Richard III* and ensured that several more of his greatest roles (from *The Entertainer* to *Dance of Death*) were immortalised on celluloid. While Gielgud led his own company with style and distinction in the 1930s, '40s and '50s, Olivier's achievement, jointly running the Old Vic Company at the New Theatre immediately after the war, and, even more so, establishing the National Theatre Company at the Old Vic in the 1960s, give him the edge as an actor-manager and theatrical entrepreneur.

In the theatre, Olivier had a breadth and power that were unrivalled in his time, but, as an actor, did Gielgud, over a longer period, have a depth and quality and authority without equal? He had a peerless grandeur. As Ralph Richardson said, 'If Johnny were to come on stage and say, "Watcher cock, I'm from the Gas Board," nobody would be convinced for a moment. But when he comes on and says, "I am the Duke of Milan", everyone believes him instantly.'

Gielgud and Olivier were both giants. You could argue that both were equally admired, in different ways, but I suspect that, by his colleagues, Gielgud was the more loved. He was probably as ambitious as Olivier, but, perhaps, less driven. By most accounts, he was certainly the sweeter and more generous of the two. Soon after Olivier had first had his extraordinary success as Richard III in 1944, Gielgud presented him with the famous sword that the great Edmund Kean had worn in the part in 1814. It had been passed, via Sir Henry Irving, into the Terry family. When Gielgud gave it to Olivier it bore a new inscription: 'This sword given him by his mother Kate Terry Gielgud, 1938, is given to Laurence Olivier by his friend John Gielgud in appreciation of his performance of Richard III at the New Theatre, 1944.' When asked, thirty-five years later, to whom he intended to bequeath the sword in the fullness of time, Olivier answered, 'No one. It's mine.'

Gielgud's instincts were always more generous. For example, some years ago, when the actor Martin Jarvis played the title role in *Richard of Bordeaux* on the radio – a role Gielgud had created and made totally his own – Sir John, who had never met him, wrote out of the blue (in his hallmark tiny handwriting that got tinier as the paragraphs narrowed and sloped sharply from left to right down the page):

Dear Martin Jarvis,

Congratulations on your splendid performance in *Bordeaux* which I listened to last night with the keenest pleasure. The whole play came over faultlessly and the version and all the performances seemed just right – and knowing the whole thing by heart and having spent two years of my life playing it, you can imagine I was hard to please.

I wish you might have the opportunity of giving it in the theatre for it seemed to me to hold up wonderfully well – and I believe the authoress would have been as satisfied as I, especially with your own performance.

All good wishes,

Most sincerely,

John Gielgud

Gielgud was generous with his praise and generous with his money. He gave financial support to young actors who needed help at the beginning of their careers and assistance to older colleagues who had fallen on hard times. Not long before Sir John's death, Kenneth Branagh said to me, 'One of the most charming things about him in relation to young actors is that he knows who we are and what we are doing. His curiosity about the current theatre and film worlds are inspiring. His knowledge of the present scene puts many of us to shame.'

A few weeks after Sir John's death, I happened to be visiting the actor Brian Blessed who was appearing at the Theatre Royal, Haymarket, Gielgud's favourite London playhouse. 'This was Gielgud's dressing room,' said my host, with pleasure and pride. 'It's vast, isn't it? Virtually a flat. I think Gielgud actually lived here during the war. I haven't seen his ghost yet, but I hope I may. Was he greater than Olivier? Does it matter? Gielgud, Olivier, Richardson, Redgrave, Wolfit – in different ways, they were all giants, great men, with wonderful presence, and huge talents. Gielgud was a lovely man. We were in the National Theatre Company on the South Bank at the same time, in different plays. He was appearing as Sir Politick Would-be in *Volpone*, an odd little part, he had a lot of feathers in his hat. Every night I used to pass him and, I'm a big fellow, so, just for fun, I used to goose him. One day Peter Hall said to me, "You can't treat Sir John like that, Brian. Stop it." So I did. At the end of the run, Sir John said to me, in that wonderful, wonderful piping voice of his, "Oh, Brian, I shall miss our backstage encounters. I rather like a bit of rough!"'

Sir John was noted for his 'naughty' sense of humour. Talking to me about the famous Terry tears – 'weak lachrymal glands', the family doctor called them – Sir John said, 'I once made a most unfortunate remark to a newspaper reporter. I told him I always burst into tears if I see a regiment marching or a queen coming.' Directing a handsome young actor, he is supposed once to have said, 'I want you to . . . I want you . . . Ohhhhh, how I want you!' At a lunch in St Tropez Gielgud asked Kenneth Tynan what a new play called *The Joint* was all about. Tynan explained: 'It's about a masochistic convict who keeps getting himself imprisoned because he likes being fucked by sadistic negro murderers.' Gielgud said, 'Well, you can't quarrel with that.'

Sir John, of course, was even more celebrated for his apparently accidental indiscretions: 'Gielgoofs' he called them. He ran into Alec Guinness in Piccadilly one day and said, 'I can't think why you want to play big parts. Why don't you stick to the little people you do so well?' Guinness protested, 'I wasn't awfully good as the Groom in *Richard II*.' 'No, I suppose you weren't.' 'And I was even worse as Aumerle.' 'Possibly. Shall we go and see a flick?'

Gielgud directed John Mills in the 1954 revival of *Charley's Aunt*. At the end of the dress rehearsal, there was dead silence from the stalls. Mills approached the edge of the stage and peered out into the auditorium. 'Johnny, are you there?' he asked. 'Yes,' replied the famous voice, 'I am.' 'Well . . . what did you think?' 'Interminable, my dear fellow, absolutely interminable.'

In 1961, rehearsing Benjamin Britten's *A Midsummer Night's Dream* at Covent Garden, he interrupted the orchestra: 'Oh, for goodness sake, do stop that racket.'

In 1964, when Richard Burton was playing in Gielgud's production of *Hamlet* on Broadway, Gielgud went backstage after the performance to collect Burton to go out to dinner: 'I'll go ahead, Richard. Come when you're better . . . I mean, when you're ready.'

In 1968, some weeks into the rehearsals for the Seneca *Oedipus* at the National Theatre, Peter Brook, as one of the many 'exercises' with which he challenged his cast, invited each of them to think of the most terrifying thing imaginable. When it came to Gielgud's turn, his response was immediate: 'We open on Tuesday!'

When John Mortimer and his wife came to dinner, bringing with them their new daughter in a carry-cot, Gielgud exclaimed: 'Why on earth didn't you leave the baby at home? Are you afraid of burglars?'

When Gielgud saw Olivier for almost the last time he is supposed to have cried out, 'Larry! You're dead! I mean . . . you're dying! I mean . . . my poor darling, you don't look at all well.'

The actor Clive Francis has fond memories of his encounters with Sir John: 'I will never forget the very first time I saw him, in his Shakespeare recital programme, *The Ages of Man* at the Theatre Royal, Brighton. I was mesmerised. He was in evening dress and stood at a lectern and yet somehow he conjured up all these characters and made them fill the stage. He was one of the reasons I became an actor. When I was thirteen or fourteen and other children were buying Acker Bilk or Frank Sinatra, I bought the record of *The Ages of Man*. Years later, when he was casting *Halfway up the Tree*, I was called back for a second audition and, as I was announced and came tentatively onto the stage, nervously anticipating this encounter with the man I admired above all others in the theatre, Sir John looked up and wailed, "Oh God, no. No, no, no, no. I'm more than certain I didn't ask for you back again."'

On one occasion, Gielgud rang the theatre critic Sheridan Morley and said, in horror, 'You'll never believe this. In America they are actually about to name a theatre after a drama critic . . . Oh my God, you are one. Goodbye.' Another of Sheridan Morley's favourite stories has Gielgud meeting Michael Redgrave in the street in 1959, shortly after Redgrave had received his knighthood. Redgrave was rumoured to have a penchant for sado-masochistic sex. Exclaimed Sir John, with a twinkle: 'Sir Michael Redgrave, I'll be bound!' This is Gielgud on Vanessa Redgrave in 1991: 'She's a marvellous actress and she never stops coming out with new plays, and she manages to find time for all that political rubbish as well.'

Peter Ustinov recalls his favourite Gielgud gaffe: 'I once saw him on a local late-night television interview in St Louis, Missouri. . . . "One final question," the interviewer said. "Sir . . . Sir Gielgud . . . did you . . . oh, you must have had . . . we all did . . . at the start of your very wonderful and very meaningful . . . let me put it this way . . . did you have someone . . . a man . . . or . . . indeed, a woman . . . at whom you could point a finger and say . . . Yes! This person helped me when I . . ."

'By now Sir John understood what was being asked of him, and he prepared to answer, disguising his dislike of all that is pretentious by perfect courtesy. "Yes, I think there was somebody who taught me a great deal at my dramatic school, and I certainly am grateful to him for his kindness and consideration toward me. His name was Claude Rains." And then, as an afterthought, he added – "I don't know what happened to him. I think he failed and went to America."'

There is an updated variation on the Claude Rains story that has Gielgud talking to Elizabeth Taylor: 'I don't know what happened to Richard Burton. I think he married some terrible film actress and had to live abroad.' I suspect that one's apocryphal. At the time of Sir John's death, several newspapers recounted the story of Gielgud at a Mansion House dinner in the late 1940s, turning to the then Prime Minister Clement Attlee and enquiring, 'Tell me, where are you living these days?' Sir John told me that the incident in fact occurred at the Falcon Hotel, Stratford-upon-Avon. Attlee was certainly there, but Gielgud actually addressed his question to the Prime Minister's daughter.

One of the earliest reported of the classic and authenticated 'Gielgoofs' has Gielgud being taken to lunch at The Ivy by Edward Knoblock, a minor playwright (he had adapted J.B. Priestley's *Good Companions*, in which Gielgud had appeared in 1931), 'a dear little man' (according to Sir John), noted for his dullness. A familiar figure passed by their table and Gielgud turned to his host: 'That man is the second biggest bore in London.' 'Who is the first?' asked his friend. 'Why, Eddie Knoblock, of course . . . Oh, I don't mean you, Eddie, the other Eddie Knoblock.' A variation on the same theme has Gielgud at a party talking about the performance of a certain foreign actress: 'Well, you can tell how dreadful she was. She was as dreadful as poor dear Athene on a very bad night.' A silence fell as the distinguished veteran actress, Athene Seyler, caught Gielgud's eye. 'Ohhh,' said Gielgud, quickly, 'Not you, Athene. No, of course, not. Another Athene, entirely.'

Several of the best of the stories (and all of the ones Sir John himself recounted) were at his own expense. In 1959, rehearsing *Five Finger Exercise*, he screamed at the cast: 'What on earth are you all doing? This is a nightmare.' 'We're doing exactly what you told us,' the actors replied. Said Sir John: 'You shouldn't have listened to me. You know I can't direct.'

The last of the reported tales has Gielgud protesting that, when he died, he did not want a memorial service at Westminster Abbey: 'It would be a dreadfully vulgar affair like Larry had and they'd get Johnny Mills to do the oration. I couldn't bear it.' In fact, because of his innate modesty, because he was not a religious man, because of his nagging anxiety about his war record, quite genuinely he neither wanted nor felt he merited interment in the Abbey. 'I've left strict instructions for no memorial service,' he said. 'They have become society functions and I don't think I have the right to be commemorated at Westminster Abbey.'

At the Abbey service for Olivier in 1989 Gielgud had read John Donne's sonnet 'Death be not proud' and had heard the Dean of Westminster's bidding: 'On Friday 20 October 1905, Sir Henry Irving was buried in Poets' Corner. Eighty-four years later to the day we come to honour the greatest actor of our time; and next year the ashes of Laurence Olivier will lie beside those of Irving and Garrick, beneath the bust of Shakespeare, and within a stone's throw of the graves of Henry V and The Lady Anne, Queen to Richard III.'

On 22 May 2000, the day Gielgud's death was announced (on what would have been Olivier's ninety-third birthday), Sir Donald Sinden wrote to the *Daily Telegraph*: 'Every actor regarded Sir John Gielgud as the leader of our profession. He spoke Shakespeare as if it were his mother tongue. (I saw his *Hamlet* of 1944 eighteen times.) For three centuries, the theatre was dominated by three great actors: David Garrick in the eighteenth, Henry Irving in the nineteenth, and John Gielgud in the twentieth. The remains of the first two are interred in Westminster Abbey. Ellen Terry once asked Irving if he wished to be buried in the Abbey, to which he somewhat immodestly replied: "I think the nation will do its duty by me." I do fervently hope that the nation will do its duty by Gielgud and that he may join his illustrious predecessors in the Abbey.'

John Gielgud was happy to have a West End theatre named after him – it seemed 'appropriate' – and felt that, if he was to be remembered at all, it should simply be for performances 'that people may have enjoyed.' 'I have only been an actor, you know,' he said to me. 'A lot of it was tosh.'

At the time of his ninety-fifth birthday, I asked a number of his friends, colleagues and admirers to pick their favourite Gielgud 'moment', the time, or the performance, they remembered best. I started with Sir Donald Sinden: 'In 1945 I had been performing with ENSA in Burma and had arrived in Bombay ready to return to the UK when John arrived with his company to perform *Hamlet* and *Blithe Spirit*. I had already seen his Hamlet nine times in London – for me, the definitive interpretation. I have now seen twenty-eight different Hamlets and none can touch his. I spent my days with the company, eating and lying on the beach. Conversation was usually theatrical tittle-tattle. Someone told me that as his company boarded the aeroplane in England, John had said, "If this plane crashes they'll have two minutes silence at The Ivy!" One evening at dinner I asked, "What are the most essential things about acting?" With hardly a pause John replied: "Feeling and timing", then, with his head erect, his eyes twinkled to the side (a favourite expression of his) as he added, "I understand it is the same in many walks of life."'

The actress Eileen Atkins told me that she played 'a piece of corn' when Sir John played Prospero in Peter Brook's production of *The Tempest* in 1957. 'I was very young, but I remember being deeply impressed that he cried so easily in it. In the reconciliation scene, Cyril Luckham, who was playing Gonzalo, used to cry too. Sir John said to him, "Cyril, don't cry. If you cry, the audience won't." Cyril protested, "But you cry, John." "Yes, I know," said Sir John, "but I'm such a silly-billy."

'When I was with John not long ago, recording *Lear* for his ninetieth birthday, he was incredible. As a person, listening to everyone as well as entertaining them. As an actor, still retaining an amazing rapidity of speech and emotional force. Oddly enough, although he has to the modern ear an incredibly posh voice and great musicality, which we don't get now, he seems very real, not at all "theatrical", and when I think of my favourite performances of his they are in modern roles. He was quite wonderful in Pinter's *No Man's Land* and, on television, as Edward Ryder in *Brideshead Revisited*.'

Richard Briers appeared with Gielgud in one of his last substantial roles for television, the Chekhov play, *Swan Song*, directed by Kenneth Branagh: 'Sir John was eighty-eight when I worked with him on the Chekhov film. The power of his personality and the enjoyment he got out of his role were striking. He entertained us with wonderful anecdotes about Irving, Forbes-Robertson and Fred Terry with total recall and would be bang up to date with what was going on in today's theatre. His enthusiasm for all things theatrical hasn't dimmed since he built his first toy theatre in 1912.

'Paul Eddington told me the story of the rehearsal of *Forty Years On* at which Sir John, playing the Headmaster, looked very unhappy, obscured at the side of the stage, surrounded by all the schoolboys. The director sensed his unease. "Where would you prefer to be Sir John?" "A little further upstage . . . towards the centre . . . under a light . . . and *on* something."

'If I had to choose one moment from his career, I'd pick Cassius in the film of *Julius Caesar*. A close-up and the line: "For we will shake him or worse days endure."'

I asked the director Peter Hall for his definitive 'Gielgud performance': 'John's was the first Hamlet I ever saw, at the beginning of the war, but if I'm only allowed to pick one performance of his it would be Angelo in Peter Brook's *Measure for Measure* at Stratford in 1950. Can't I have two? I want two because I have to choose Spooner in *No Man's Land* at the National in the mid-seventies.'

Sir Alec Guinness, who was born exactly ten years after Gielgud and died just ten weeks after him, used to joke that he found it profoundly irritating when 'John G would scamper down the stairs to assist me in clambering up them'. Guinness never forgot his early debt to Gielgud or the magic of the man. He sent me his thoughts in 1999: 'It is sixty-five years since I first worked for him, playing Osric in his definitive *Hamlet* of 1934, and although he has lost none of his authority and charm in the intervening years it is impossible to convey to a younger generation the glamour and theatrical innovations he represented. He has straddled the English theatre for most of this century as the exemplary actor, his head thrown back as if peering beyond us, his eye clear as an April morning, his voice always instantly recognisable and thrilling. In younger days an exotic whiff of Cypriot cigarettes preceded him as he entered the stage door, his smart black trilby hat tilted over his nose; and his manner was a rather unsettling combination of courtesy, exasperation and professional impatience, as if nothing must impede his progress to his dressing room and the stage. He was hero-worshipped by many young actors like myself who copied, in the cheapest form possible, his outward trappings without being able to emulate the inner man.

'If forced to choose just one performance out of so many, I think it would be his Mercutio, from later that same season at the New Theatre, when he and Olivier alternated Mercutio and Romeo.'

One of the guests at the lunch I organised to mark Sir John's eightieth birthday was the actress Constance Cummings. She picked his Macbeth as the most memorable of his performances: 'I think John and Shakespeare have much in common. The few descriptions we have of Shakespeare's character from his contemporaries assure us he was a man of wit . . . of a sweet disposition . . . always a pleasant, courteous companion . . . he was highly esteemed by his contemporaries in and out of the theatre . . . all this is said of John. As author and as actor they share the mysterious gift of using words to take us into realms of awareness and understanding where paraphrase is dumb.'

I once asked Sir John for his favourite speech in Shakespeare. 'Where to begin?' he sighed. 'Where to end?' I said. 'That's much easier,' he smiled, and put down his glass, pushed it across the table, half-closed his eyes and, in that unmistakable voice, said, without pause:

> Our revels now are ended. These our actors,
> As I foretold you, were all spirits and
> Are melted into air, into thin air:
> And, like the baseless fabric of this vision,
> The cloud-capped towers, the gorgeous palaces,
> The solemn temples, the great globe itself,
> Yea, all which it inherit, shall dissolve
> And, like this insubstantial pageant faded,
> Leave not a rack behind. We are such stuff
> As dreams are made on, and our little life
> Is rounded with a sleep.

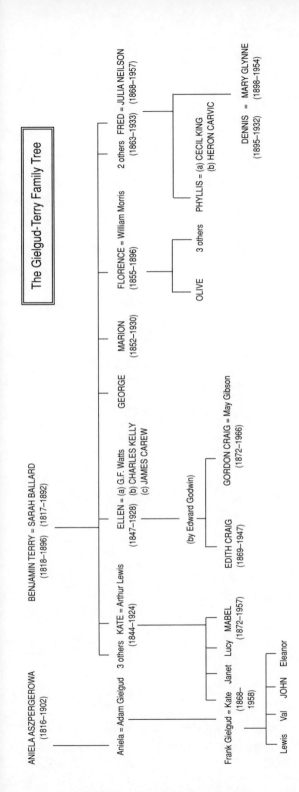

The Gielgud-Terry Family Tree

Names in capital letters indicate members of the family associated with the theatre.

Stage Chronology · JOHN GIELGUD · Actor and Director

Theatre/Year	Play	Author	Role	Director
1921				
Old Vic	Henry V	Shakespeare	Herald	Robert Atkins
1922				
Old Vic	Peer Gynt	Ibsen	Walk on	Robert Atkins
Old Vic	King Lear	Shakespeare	Walk on	Robert Atkins
Old Vic	Wat Tyler	Halcott Glover	Walk on	Robert Atkins
On tour	The Wheel	J.B. Fagan	Lieut. Manners	J.B. Fagan
1923				
Regent	The Insect Play	Josef and Karel Capek	Felix, the Poet Butterfly	Nigel Playfair
Regent	Robert E. Lee	John Drinkwater	Aide de Camp	Nigel Playfair and John Drinkwater
Comedy	Charley's Aunt	Brandon Thomas	Charley	Amy Brandon-Thomas
1924				
Oxford Playhouse	Captain Brassbound's Conversion	Bernard Shaw	Johnson	Reginald Denham
Oxford Playhouse	Love for Love	William Congreve	Valentine	Reginald Denham
Oxford Playhouse	Mr Pim Passes By	A.A. Milne	Brian Strange	J.B. Fagan
Oxford Playhouse	She Stoops to Conquer	Oliver Goldsmith	Young Marlow	Reginald Denham
Oxford Playhouse	Monna Vanna	Maurice Maeterlinck	Prinzevalle	Reginald Denham

· 165 ·

Theatre/Year	Play	Author	Role	Director
RADA	Romeo and Juliet	Shakespeare	Paris	H.K. Ayliff
Regent	Romeo and Juliet	Shakespeare	Romeo	J.B. Fagan
RADA	The Return Half	John van Druten	John Sherry	J.B. Fagan
Oxford Playhouse	Candida	Bernard Shaw	Marchbanks	J.B. Fagan
Oxford Playhouse	Deirdre of the Sorrows	J.M. Synge	Naisi	J.B. Fagan
Oxford Playhouse	A Collection Will Be Made	Arthur Eckersley	Paul Roget	J.B. Fagan
Oxford Playhouse	Everybody's Husband	Gilbert Cannan	A Domino	J.B. Fagan
Oxford Playhouse	The Cradle Song	Gregorio Martinez Sierra	Antonio	J.B. Fagan
Oxford Playhouse	John Gabriel Borkman	Ibsen	Erhart	J.B. Fagan
Oxford Playhouse	His Widow's Husband	Jacinto Benavente	Florencio	J.B. Fagan
Oxford Playhouse	Madame Pepita	Gregorio Martinez Sierra	Augusto	J.B. Fagan

1925

Theatre/Year	Play	Author	Role	Director
Oxford Playhouse	A Collection Will Be Made	Arthur Eckersley	Paul Roget	J.B. Fagan
Oxford Playhouse	Smith	Somerset Maugham	Algernon	J.B. Fagan
Oxford Playhouse	The Cherry Orchard	Chekhov	Trofimov	J.B. Fagan
RADA	The Nature of the Evidence	Harold Peacey	Ted Hewitt	Guy Pelham Boulton
Aldwych (Phoenix Society)	The Orphan	Thomas Otway	Castalio	Allan Wade
Lyric, Hammersmith	The Cherry Orchard	Chekhov	Trofimov	J.B. Fagan
Royalty	The Cherry Orchard	Chekhov	Trofimov	J.B. Fagan
Little	The Vortex	Noël Coward	Nicky Lancaster	Noël Coward
Oxford Playhouse	The Lady from the Sea	Ibsen	A Stranger	J.B. Fagan
Oxford Playhouse	The Man with the Flower in His Mouth	Luigi Pirandello	Title part	J.B. Fagan

· 166 ·

Theatre/Year	Play	Author	Role	Director
Little	The Seagull	Chekhov	Konstantin	A.E. Filmer
New Oxford (Phoenix Society)	Dr Faustus	Christopher Marlowe	Good Angel	Allan Wade
Little	Gloriana	Gwen John	Sir John Harrington	George Owen
Prince's (Play Actors)	L'Ecole des Cocottes	Paul Armant and Marcel Gerbidon	Robert	H.M. Harwood
1926				
Savoy (matinees)	The Tempest	Shakespeare	Ferdinand	Henry Baynton
RADA	Sons and Fathers	Allan Monkhouse	Richard Southern	Milton Rosmer
Barnes	Three Sisters	Chekhov	Tuzenbach	Theodore Komisarjevsky
Barnes	Katerina	I.N. Andreyev	Georg	Theodore Komisarjevsky
Garrick	The Lady of the Camellias	A. Dumas *fils*	Armand	Sydney Bland
Court (300 Club)	Confession	W.F. Casey	Wilfred Marlay	Reginald Denham
New	The Constant Nymph	Margaret Kennedy and Basil Dean	Lewis Dodd	Basil Dean
1927				
Apollo (Lyceum Club Stage Society)	Othello	Shakespeare	Cassio	A.E. Filmer
Strand (Stage Society)	The Great God Brown	Eugene O'Neill	Dion Anthony	Peter Godfrey
1928				
Majestic, New York	The Patriot	Alfred Neumann	The Tsarevich	Gilbert Miller

Theatre/Year	Play	Author	Role	Director
Wyndham's (matinees)	Ghosts	Ibsen	Oswald	Peter Godfrey
Arts	Ghosts	Ibsen	Oswald	Peter Godfrey
Arts (matinees)	Prejudice	Mercedes de Acosta	Jacob Slovak	Leslie Banks
Globe	Holding Out the Apple	B. Wynne-Bower	Dr Gerald Marlowe	Leon M. Lion
Shaftesbury	The Skull	B.J. McOwen and H.E. Humphrey	Captain Allenby	Victor Morley
Court	The Lady From Alfaqueque	Serafin and Joaquin Alvarez Quintero	Felipe Rivas	James Whale
Court	Fortunato	Serafin and Joaquin Alvarez Quintero	Alberto	James Whale
Strand	Out of the Sea	Don Marquis	John Martin	Campbell Gullan and Henry Oscar
1929				
Arts	The Seagull	Chekhov	Konstantin	A.E. Filmer
Little	Red Dust	V.M. Kirchow and A.V. Ouspensky	Fedor	Frank Vernon
Prince of Wales (Sunday Play Society)	Hunter's Moon	Sophus Michaelis	Paul de Tressailles	Leslie Faber
Garrick	The Lady with the Lamp	Reginald Berkeley	Henry Tremayne	Leslie Banks and Edith Evans
Arts	Red Sunday	Hubert Griffith	Bronstein (Trotsky)	Theodore Komisarjevsky
Old Vic	Romeo and Juliet	Shakespeare	Romeo	Harcourt Williams
Old Vic	The Merchant of Venice	Shakespeare	Antonio	Harcourt Williams

· 168 ·

Theatre/Year	Play	Author	Role	Director
Old Vic	The Imaginary Invalid	Molière	Cléante	Harcourt Williams
Old Vic	Richard II	Shakespeare	Richard II	Harcourt Williams
Old Vic	A Midsummer Night's Dream	Shakespeare	Oberon	Harcourt Williams
1930				
Old Vic	Julius Caesar	Shakespeare	Mark Antony	Harcourt Williams
Old Vic	As You Like It	Shakespeare	Orlando	Harcourt Williams
Old Vic	Androcles and the Lion	Bernard Shaw	The Emperor	Harcourt Williams with Edward Carrick
Old Vic	Macbeth	Shakespeare	Macbeth	Harcourt Williams
Old Vic	The Man with the Flower in his Mouth	Luigi Pirandello	Title part	Harcourt Williams
Old Vic	Hamlet	Shakespeare	Hamlet	Harcourt Williams
Queen's	Hamlet	Shakespeare	Hamlet	Harcourt Williams
Lyric, Hammersmith	The Importance of Being Earnest	Oscar Wilde	John Worthing	Nigel Playfair
Old Vic	Henry IV, Part I	Shakespeare	Hotspur	Harcourt Williams
Old Vic	The Tempest	Shakespeare	Prospero	Harcourt Williams
Old Vic	The Jealous Wife	George Colman	Lord Trinket	Harcourt Williams
Old Vic	Antony and Cleopatra	Shakespeare	Antony	Harcourt Williams
1931				
Sadler's Wells	Twelfth Night	Shakespeare	Malvolio	Harcourt Williams
Old Vic	Arms and the Man	Bernard Shaw	Sergius	Harcourt Williams

Theatre/Year	Play	Author	Role	Director
Old Vic	Much Ado About Nothing	Shakespeare	Benedick	Harcourt Williams
Old Vic	King Lear	Shakespeare	Lear	Harcourt Williams
His Majesty's	The Good Companions	J.B. Priestley and Edward Knoblock	Inigo Jollifant	Julian Wylie
1932				
New, Oxford (OUDS)	Romeo and Juliet	Shakespeare	Director	Theodore Komisarjevsky
Criterion	Musical Chairs	Ronald Mackenzie	Joseph Schindler	
St Martin's	Strange Orchestra	Rodney Ackland	Director	
Old Vic	The Merchant of Venice	Shakespeare	Director	
1933				
New	Richard of Bordeaux	Gordon Daviot	Richard, and co-Director	
Wyndham's	Sheppey	Somerset Maugham	Director	
1934				
Shaftesbury	Spring 1600	Emlyn Williams	Director, and co-Producer	
New	Queen of Scots	Gordon Daviot	Director	
Wyndham's	The Maitlands	Ronald Mackenzie	Roger Maitland	Theodore Komisarjevsky
New	Hamlet	Shakespeare	Hamlet, and Director	
1935				
New	The Old Ladies	Rodney Ackland	Director	
New	Noah	André Obey	Noah	Michel Saint-Denis
New	Romeo and Juliet	Shakespeare	Mercutio, and Director	

Theatre/Year	Play	Author	Role	Director
New	Romeo and Juliet	Shakespeare	Romeo, and Director	
1936				
OUDS	Richard II	Shakespeare	Director	
New	The Seagull	Chekhov	Trigorin	Theodore Komisarjevsky
Alexandra, Toronto	Hamlet	Shakespeare	Hamlet	Guthrie McClintic
St James's, New York	Hamlet	Shakespeare	Hamlet	Guthrie McClintic
1937				
Queen's	He Was Born Gay	Emlyn Williams	Mason, co-Director, and co-Producer	
Queen's	Richard II	Shakespeare	Richard, Director and Producer	
Queen's	The School for Scandal	Sheridan	Joseph Surface, and Producer	Tyrone Guthrie
1938				
Queen's	Three Sisters	Chekhov	Vershinin, and Producer	Michel Saint-Denis
Queen's	The Merchant of Venice	Shakespeare	Shylock, co-Director and Producer	
Ambassadors'	Spring Meeting	M.J. Farrell and John Perry	Director	
Queen's	Dear Octopus	Dodie Smith	Nicholas	Glen Byam Shaw
1939				
Globe	The Importance of Being Earnest	Oscar Wilde	John Worthing, and Director	

Theatre/Year	Play	Author	Role	Director
Globe	Rhondda Roundabout	Jack Jones	Director	
Lyceum	Hamlet	Shakespeare	Hamlet, and Director	
Elsinore Castle	Hamlet	Shakespeare	Hamlet, and Director	
Globe	The Importance of Being Earnest	Oscar Wilde	John Worthing, and Director	
1940				
Haymarket	The Beggar's Opera	John Gay	Director	
Old Vic	King Lear	Shakespeare	Lear	Lewis Casson and Harley Granville Barker
Old Vic	The Tempest	Shakespeare	Prospero	George Devine and Marius Goring
Globe and ENSA tour	Fumed Oak	Noël Coward	Henry Crow, and Director	
Globe and ENSA tour	Hands Across the Sea	Noël Coward	Peter Gilpin, and Director	
Globe and ENSA tour	Hard Luck Story	Chekhov	Old Actor, and Director	
1941				
Globe	Dear Brutus	J.M. Barrie	Will Dearth, and Director	
Apollo	Ducks and Drakes	M.J. Farrell	Director	
1942				
Tour	Macbeth	Shakespeare	Macbeth, and Director	
Piccadilly	Macbeth	Shakespeare	Macbeth, and Director	

Theatre/Year	Play	Author	Role	Director
Phoenix	The Importance of Being Earnest	Oscar Wilde	John Worthing, and Director	
1943				
Haymarket	The Doctor's Dilemma	Bernard Shaw	Louis Dubedat	Irene Hentschel
Phoenix and Haymarket	Love for Love	Congreve	Valentine, and Director	
Westminster	Landslide	Dorothy Albertyn and David Peel	Director	
1944				
Apollo	The Cradle Song	Gregorio Martinez Sierra	Director	
Lyric	Crisis in Heaven	Eric Linklater	Director	
Phoenix	The Last of Summer	Kate O'Brien and John Perry	Director	George Rylands
Tour	Hamlet	Shakespeare	Hamlet	
Tour	Love for Love	Congreve	Valentine, and Director	
Tour	The Circle	Somerset Maugham	Arnold Champion-Cheney	William Armstong
Haymarket	The above three plays in repertoire			
1945				
Haymarket	A Midsummer Night's Dream	Shakespeare	Oberon	Nevill Coghill
Haymarket	The Duchess of Malfi	John Webster	Ferdinand	George Rylands
Haymarket	Lady Windermere's Fan	Oscar Wilde	Director	

Theatre/Year	Play	Author	Role	Director
Far East Tour, ENSA	Hamlet	Shakespeare	Hamlet, and Director	
Far East Tour, ENSA	Blithe Spirit	Noël Coward	Charles Condomine, and Director	Anthony Quayle
1946				
New and Globe	Crime and Punishment	Rodney Ackland	Raskolnikoff	
1947				
Royale, New York	The Importance of Being Earnest	Oscar Wilde	John Worthing, and Director	
US tour	Love for Love	Congreve	Valentine, and Director	
National, New York	Medea	Euripides	Jason, and Director	
National, New York	Crime and Punishment	Rodney Ackland	Raskolnikoff	Anthony Quayle
1948				
Haymarket	The Glass Menagerie	Tennessee Williams	Director	
Globe	Medea	Euripides	Director	
Globe	The Return of the Prodigal	St John Hankin	Eustace Jackson	Peter Glenville
1949				
Haymarket	The Heiress	Ruth and Augustus Goetz	Director	
Memorial, Stratford	Much Ado About Nothing	Shakespeare	Director	
Globe	The Lady's Not For Burning	Christopher Fry	Thomas Mendip, and Director	
Apollo	Treasure Hunt	M.J. Farrell and John Perry	Director	

Theatre/Year	Play	Author	Role	Director
1950				
Lyric, Hammersmith	The Boy with a Cart	Christopher Fry	Director	
Lyric, Hammersmith	Shall We Join the Ladies?	J.M. Barrie	Director	
Memorial, Stratford	Measure for Measure	Shakespeare	Angelo	Peter Brook
Memorial, Stratford	Julius Caesar	Shakespeare	Cassius	Anthony Quayle and Michael Langham
Memorial, Stratford	Much Ado About Nothing	Shakespeare	Benedick, and Director	
Memorial, Stratford	King Lear	Shakespeare	Lear, and co-Director	
1951				
Royale, New York	The Lady's Not For Burning	Christopher Fry	Thomas Mendip, and Director	
Phoenix	The Winter's Tale	Shakespeare	Leontes	Peter Brook
1952				
Phoenix	Much Ado About Nothing	Shakespeare	Benedick, and Director	
Memorial, Stratford	Macbeth	Shakespeare	Director	
Lyric, Hammersmith	Richard II	Shakespeare	Director	
1953				
Lyric, Hammersmith	The Way of the World	Congreve	Mirabell, and Director	
Lyric, Hammersmith	Venice Preserv'd	Thomas Otway	Jaffier	Peter Brook
Bulawayo	Richard II	Shakespeare	Richard, and Director	
Haymarket	A Day by the Sea	N.C. Hunter	Julian Anson, and Director	

Theatre/Year	Play	Author	Role	Director
1954				
New	Charley's Aunt	Brandon Thomas	Director	
Lyric, Hammersmith	The Cherry Orchard	Chekhov, adapted John Gielgud	Director	
1955				
Memorial, Stratford	Twelfth Night	Shakespeare	Director	
European Tour	King Lear	Shakespeare	Lear, and co-Director	
Palace	Much Ado About Nothing	Shakespeare	Benedick, and Director	
Palace	King Lear	Shakespeare	Lear, and co-Director	
European tour	The two plays above			
1956				
Haymarket	The Chalk Garden	Enid Bagnold	Director	
Globe	Nude with Violin	Noël Coward	Sebastian, and Director	
1957				
Covent Garden	The Trojans	Berlioz	Director	
Memorial, Stratford	The Tempest	Shakespeare	Prospero	Peter Brook
Tour	The Ages of Man	Shakespeare	Anthology	
Drury Lane	The Tempest	Shakespeare	Prospero	Peter Brook
1958				
Globe	The Potting Shed	Graham Greene	James Callifer	Michael MacOwan

· 176 ·

Theatre/Year	Play	Author	Role	Director
Globe	Variation on a Theme	Terence Rattigan	Director	Michael Benthall
Old Vic	Henry VIII	Shakespeare	Wolsey	
Tour of USA, Canada	The Ages of Man	Shakespeare	Anthology	
46th Street, New York	The Ages of Man	Shakespeare	Anthology	
1959				
Globe	The Complaisant Lover	Graham Greene	Director	
Queen's	The Ages of Man	Shakespeare	Anthology	
US tour	Much Ado About Nothing	Shakespeare	Director	
Music Box, New York	Five Finger Exercise	Peter Shaffer	Director	
1960				
Phoenix	The Last Joke	Enid Bagnold	Prince Ferdinand	Glen Byam Shaw
1961				
Covent Garden	A Midsummer Night's Dream	Michael Tippett	Director	
ANTA, New York	Big Fish, Little Fish	Hugh Wheeler	Director	
Globe	Dazzling Prospect	M.J. Farrell and John Perry	Director	Franco Zeffirelli
Royal Shakespeare, Stratford	Othello	Shakespeare	Othello	Franco Zeffirelli
Aldwych	The Cherry Orchard	Chekhov	Gaev	Michel Saint-Denis
1962				
Haymarket	The School for Scandal	Sheridan	Director	
Haymarket	The School for Scandal	Sheridan	Joseph Surface and, Director	

· 177 ·

Theatre/Year	Play	Author	Role	Director
Majestic, New York	The School for Scandal	Sheridan	Joseph Surface and, Director	
1963				
Majestic, New York	The Ages of Man			
Haymarket	The Ides of March	Thornton Wilder	Caesar, and co-Director	
1964				
Lunt-Fontanne, New York	Hamlet	Shakespeare	Ghost (recorded), and Director	
World tour	The Ages of Man			
Billy Rose, New York	Tiny Alice	Edward Albee	Julian	Alan Schneider
1965				
Phoenix	Ivanov	Chekhov, adapted John Gielgud	Ivanov, and Director	
1966				
US tour	Ivanov	Chekhov, adapted John Gielgud	Ivanov, and Director	
Schubert, New York	Ivanov	Chekhov, adapted John Gielgud	Ivanov, and Director	
1967				
US tour	The Ages of Man			

Theatre/Year	Play	Author	Role	Director
Queen's	Halfway Up the Tree	Peter Ustinov	Director	
Old Vic (NT)	Tartuffe	Molière	Orgon	Tyrone Guthrie
1968				
Old Vic (NT)	Oedipus	Seneca, adapted Ted Hughes	Oedipus	Peter Brook
Coliseum	Don Giovanni	Mozart	Director	
Apollo	Forty Years On	Alan Bennett	Headmaster	Patrick Garland
1970				
Lyric	The Battle of Shrivings	Peter Shaffer	Sir Gideon Petrie	Peter Hall
Royal Court	Home	David Storey	Harry	Lindsay Anderson
Morosco, New York	Home	David Storey	Harry	Lindsay Anderson
1971				
Chichester	Caesar and Cleopatra	Bernard Shaw	Caesar	Robin Phillips
1972				
Royal Court	Veterans	Charles Wood	Sir Geoffrey Kendle	Ronald Eyre
Queen's	Private Lives	Noël Coward	Director	
1973				
Albery	The Constant Wife	Somerset Maugham	Director	
1974				
Old Vic (NT)	The Tempest	Shakespeare	Prospero	Peter Hall

Theatre/Year	Play	Author	Role	Director
Royal Court	Bingo	Edward Bond	Shakespeare	Jane Howell and John Dove
1975				
Old Vic (NT)	No Man's Land	Harold Pinter	Spooner	Peter Hall
Albery	The Gay Lord Quex	Arthur Pinero	Director	
Wyndham's (NT)	No Man's Land	Harold Pinter	Spooner	Peter Hall
1976				
Old Vic (NT)	Tribute to the Lady	devised Val May		Val May
Lyttelton	No Man's Land	Harold Pinter	Spooner	Peter Hall
Longacre, New York	No Man's Land	Harold Pinter	Spooner	Peter Hall
1977				
Lyttelton	No Man's Land	Harold Pinter	Spooner	Peter Hall
Olivier	Julius Caesar	Shakespeare	Caesar	John Schlesinger
Olivier	Volpone	Ben Jonson	Sir Politick Would-Be	Peter Hall
Cottesloe	Half-Life	Julian Mitchell	Sir Noel Cunliffe	Waris Hussein
1978				
Duke of York's	Half-Life	Julian Mitchell	Sir Noel Cunliffe	Waris Hussein
1987				
Apollo	The Best of Friends	Hugh Whitemore	Sir Sydney Cockerell	James Roose-Evans

Film and Television Chronology · Major Roles

Date	Film (TV)	Role	Director
1924	Who is the Man?	Daniel	Walter Summers
1929	The Clue of the New Pin	Rex Trasmere	Arthur Maude
1932	Insult	Henri Dubois	Harry Lachman
1933	The Good Companions	Inigo Jollifant	Victor Saville
1936	The Secret Agent	Edgar Brodie	Alfred Hitchcock
1941	The Prime Minister	Benjamin Disraeli	Thorold Dickinson
1953	Julius Caesar	Cassius	Joseph Mankiewicz
1955	Richard III	Clarence	Laurence Olivier
1957	Around the World in 80 Days	Foster	Michael Anderson
	The Barretts of Wimpole Street	Edward Moulton Barrett	Sidney Franklin
	Saint Joan	Warwick	Otto Preminger
1959	A Day by the Sea (TV)	Julian Anson	
	The Browning Version (TV)	Andrew Crocker Harris	
	The Rehearsal (TV)	The Count	
1963	Becket	Louis VII	Peter Glenville
1964	The Loved One	Sir Francis Hinsley	Tony Richardson
1966	Chimes at Midnight	Henry IV	Orson Welles
	Alice in Wonderland (TV)	Mock Turtle	Jonathan Miller
	The Mayfly and the Frog (TV)	Gabriel Kantara	
	From Chekhov with Love (TV)	Chekhov	
1967	Mister Sebastian	Head of British Intelligence	David Greene
	The Charge of the Light Brigade	Lord Raglan	Tony Richardson

Date	Film (TV)	Role	Director
1968	The Shoes of the Fisherman	The Elder Pope	Michael Anderson
	Saint Joan (TV)	The Inquisitor	
	Oh! What a Lovely War	Count Berchtold	Richard Attenborough
1969	In Good King Charles's Golden Days (TV)	King Charles	
	Conversation at Night (TV)	The Writer	Rudolf Cartier
1970	Julius Caesar	Caesar	Stuart Burge
	Eagle in a Cage	Lord Sissal	Fielder Cook
	Hassan (TV)	The Caliph	
	Hamlet (TV)	The Ghost	
1972	Lost Horizon	Chang	Charles Jarrott
1974	11 Harrowhouse	Meecham	Aram Avakian
	Gold	Farrell	Peter Hunt
	Murder on the Orient Express	Beddoes	Sidney Lumet
	Galileo	Cardinal	Joseph Losey
1975	Shades of Greene: Special Duties (TV)	Mr Ferraro	Alastair Reid
1976	Edward VII (TV)	Disraeli	John Gorrie
	The Picture of Dorian Gray (TV)	Lord Wotton	John Gorrie
	Aces High	Headmaster	Jack Gold
	Caesar and Cleopatra	Caesar	
	Joseph Andrews	Doctor	Tony Richardson
1977	Providence	Clive Langham	Alain Resnais
	Heartbreak House (TV)	Captain Shotover	Cedric Messina
	A Portrait of the Artist as a Young Man	Preacher	Joseph Strick
	The Grand Inquisitor (TV)	Title role	Richard Argent

Date	Film (TV)	Role	Director
1978	No Man's Land (TV)	Spooner	Julian Amyes
	Richard II	John of Gaunt	David Giles
	The Cherry Orchard (TV)	Gaev	
	Les Miserables	Valjean's father	Glenn Jordan
	Murder by Decree	Lord Salisbury	Bob Clark
	Romeo and Juliet (TV)	Chorus	Alvin Rakoff
1979	The Conductor	Title role	Andrzej Wajda
	The Human Factor	Brigadier Tomlinson	Otto Preminger
	Caligula	Nerva	Tinto Brass
	Why Didn't They Ask Evans? (TV)		John Davies
	Tales of the Unexpected: Neck (TV)	Jelks	Christopher Miles
1980	The Elephant Man	Carr Gomm	David Lynch
	Tales of the Unexpected: The Parson's Pleasure (TV)	Cyril Boggis	John Bruce
	Sphinx	Abdu	Franklin J. Schaffner
	Seven Dials of Mystery (TV)	Marquis of Caterham	Tony Wharmby
1981	Omar Mukhtar: The Lion of the Desert	Sharif El Gariani	Moustapha Akkad
	Arthur	Hobson	Steve Gordon
	Chariots of Fire	Master of Trinity	Hugh Hudson
	The Formula	Dr Esau	John G. Avildsen
	Priest of Love	Herbert G. Muskett	Christopher Miles
	Brideshead Revisited (TV)	Edward Ryder	Charles Sturridge and Michael Lindsay-Hogg
1982	Marco Polo	Doge	Giuliano Montaldo
	The Critic (TV)	Lord Burleigh	Don Taylor
	Hunchback of Notre Dame (TV)	Torturer	Michael Tuchner

Date	Film (TV)	Role	Director
	Inside the Third Reich (TV)	Speer's father	Marvin J. Chomsky
	Buddenbrooks	Narrator	Franz Peter Wirth
1983	Wagner	Pfistermeister	Tony Palmer
	Gandhi	Lord Irwin	Richard Attenborough
	Scandalous	Uncle Willie	Rob Cohen
	The Wicked Lady	Hogarth	Michael Winner
	The Vatican Story aka The Vatican Pimpernel aka The Scarlet & The Black	Pope Pius VII	Jerry London
	Invitation to the Wedding	Clyde Ormiston	Joseph Brooks
	The Master of Ballantrae (TV)	Lord Dumsdeer	Douglas Hickox
1984	The Far Pavilions (TV)	Cavagnari	Peter Duffell
	The Shooting Party	Cornelius Cardew	Alan Bridges
	Frankenstein (TV)	De Lacey	James Ormerod
	Camille (TV)	The Duke	Desmond Davis
	Plenty	Sir Leonard Darwin	Fred Schepisi
	Romance on the Orient Express	Charles Woodward	Lawrence Gordon Clark
1985	Leave All Fair	John Middleton Murray	John Reid
	Time after Time (TV)	Jasper Swift	Bill Hays
	The Theban Plays by Sophocles: Oedipus the King (TV)	Teiresias	Don Taylor
1986	The Theban Plays by Sophocles: Antigone (TV)	Teiresias	Don Taylor
	The Whistle Blower	Sir Adrian Chapple	Simon Langton
	The Canterville Ghost	Sir Simon de Canterville	Paul Bogart
	War & Remembrance (TV)	Dr Aaron Jastrow	Dan Curtis
1987	Appointment with Death	Colonel Carbury	Michael Winner

· 184 ·

Date	Film (TV)	Role	Director
	Bluebeard	Bluebeard	Fabio Carpi
	Arthur II	Hobson	Bud Yorkin
	Quartermaine's Terms (TV)	Loomis	Bill Hays
1988	Getting it Right	Sir Gordon Munday	Randal Kleiser
	A Man for All Seasons (TV)	Cardinal Wolsey	Charlton Heston
1989	A Summer's Lease (TV)	Haverford Downs	Martyn Friend
1990	Prospero's Books	Prospero	Peter Greenaway
	Strauss Dynasty		Marvyn J. Chomsky
	Shining Through	Konrad Friedrichs	David Seltzer
	Loser Takes All		James Scott
	A TV Dante (TV)	Virgil	Peter Greenaway
1991	The Best of Friends (TV)	Sir Sydney Cockerell	James Roose-Evans
	The Power of One	Headmaster St John	John G. Avildsen
1992	Swan Song	Vasily Svetlovidov	Kenneth Branagh
1993	Inspector Morse: Twilight of the Gods (TV)	Lord Hinksey	Herbert Wise
	Under the Hammer (TV)		Robert Tronson
	Lovejoy: The Lost Colony (TV)	Lord Wakering	Geoffrey Sax
1994	First Night	Oswald	Jerry Zucker
	Haunted	Dr Doyle	Lewis Gilbert
	Summer's Day Dream (TV)		
	Scarlett (TV)	Pierre Robillard	John Erman
	Inspector Alleyne (TV)	Percival Pyke Period	Martyn Friend
1995	Shine	Cecil Parkes	Scott Hicks
	Portrait of a Lady		

Date	Film (TV)	Role	Director
1995	Shine	Cecil Parkes	Scott Hicks
	Portrait of Lady	Mr Touchet	Jane Campion
	Words from Jerusalem (TV)	Narrator	
	Gulliver's Travels (TV)	Professor of Sunlight	Charles Sturridge
1996	Dance to the Music of Time (TV)	St John Clarke	Alvin Rakoff and Christopher Morahan
1997	The Tichborne Claimant	Cockburn	David Yates
1998	Merlin (TV)	King Constant	Steve Barron
1999	Catastrophe (TV)		David Mamet

BIBLIOGRAPHY

Agate, James, *Brief Chronicles* (1943), *Red Letter Nights* (1945), *The Contemporary Theatre* (1946), *The Selective Ego* (edited by Tim Beaumont, 1976)

Anthony, Gordon, *John Gielgud, Camera Studies by Gordon Anthony with an Introduction by Michel Saint-Denis* (1938)

Baxter, Keith, *My Sentiments Exactly* (1998)

Beaton, Cecil, *The Selected Diaries of Cecil Beaton* (edited by Richard Buckle, 1979)

Bennett, Alan, *Writing Home* (1994)

Bishop, George W., *My Betters* (1957)

Black, Kitty, *Upper Circle* (1984)

Bloom, Claire, *Limelight and After* (1982)

Bogarde, Dirk, *An Orderly Man* (1983)

Brandreth, Gyles, *Great Theatrical Disasters* (1982), *John Gielgud – A Celebration* (1984, 1994), *Under the Jumper* (1993), *Breaking the Code – Westminster Diaries* (1999)

Brook, Peter, *Threads of Time* (1998)

Burton, Hal (ed.), *Great Acting* (1967)

Casson, John, *Lewis and Sybil – A Memoir* (1972)

Coward, Noel, *The Noel Coward Diaries* (edited by Graham Payn and Sheridan Morley, 1982)

Culver, Roland, *Not Quite a Gentleman* (1979)

Curtis, Anthony, *The Rise and Fall of the Matinee Idol* (1974)

Farjeon, Herbert, *The Shakespearean Scene* (1949)

Findlater, Richard, *These Our Actors* (1983)

Fordham, Hallam, *John Gielgud* (1952)

Francis, Clive, *Sir John – The Many Faces of Gielgud* (1994)

Funke, Lewis, and Booth, John E., *Actors Talk about Acting* (1961)

Gielgud, John, *Early Stages* (1939), *Stage Directions* (1963), *Distinguished Company* (1972), *An Actor in his Time* (1979), *Backward Glances* (1989)

Gilder, Rosamond, *John Gielgud's Hamlet* (1937)

Greenaway, Peter, *Prospero's Books* (1991)

Guinness, Alec, *Blessings in Disguise* (1985)

Guthrie, Tyrone, *A Life in the Theatre* (1959)

Hall, Peter, *Peter Hall's Diaries* (edited by John Goodwin, 1983), *Making an Exhibition of Myself* (1993, 2000)

Harwood, Ronald (ed.), *The Ages of Gielgud* (1984)

Hayman, Ronald, *John Gielgud* (1971)

Hobson, Harold, *Theatre in Britain – A Personal View* (1984)

Huggett, Richard, *Binkie Beaumont* (1989)

Kauffmann, Stanley, *Before My Eyes* (1974)

Mander, Raymond, and Mitchenson, Joe, *Hamlet Through the Ages* (1952)

Marowitz, C., Milne, T., and Hale, O., *The Encore Reader* (1965)

Mason, James, *Before I Forget* (1981)

Mills, John, *Up in the Clouds, Gentlemen Please* (1980)

Nichols, Beverley, *The Unforgiving Minute* (1978)

Nicolson, Harold, *Diaries and Letters 1930–39* (edited by Nigel Nicolson, 1966)

Olivier, Laurence, *Confessions of an Actor* (1982), *On Acting* (1986)

Quayle, Anthony, *A Time to Speak* (1990)

Redfield, William, *Letters from an Actor* (1966)

Redgrave, Michael, *In My Mind's Eye* (1983)

Richardson, Tony, *Long Distance Runner* (1993)

Sinden, Donald, *A Touch of the Memoirs* (1982)

Speaight, Robert, *Shakespeare on Stage* (1973)

Stern, Richard L., *John Gielgud directs Richard Burton in Hamlet* (1967)

Trewin, J.C, *A Play Tonight* (1952), *The Theatre since 1900* (1951)

——, Mander, Raymond, and Mitchenson, Joe, *The Gay Twenties – A Decade in the Theatre* (1958)

Tynan, Kenneth, *He that Plays the King* (1950), *Curtains* (1961), *The Sound of Two Hands Clapping* (1975), *Letters* (edited by Kathleen Tynan, 1994)

Ustinov, Peter, *Dear Me* (1977)

Welles, Orson, and Bogdanovich, Peter, *This is Orson Welles* (1993)

Williams, Emlyn, *Emlyn* (1973)

Williams, Harcourt, *Four Years at the Old Vic* (1935), *Old Vic Saga* (1949)

Williams, Tennessee, *Memoirs* (1976)

Williamson, Audrey, *Old Vic Drama* (1948)

Wolfit, Donald, *First Interval* (1954)

INDEX